RECIPE
FOR
SUCCESS

RECIPE
FOR
SUCCESS

An Insider's Guide to Bringing Your Natural Food to Market

Abigail Steinberg

AMACOM

American Management Association

New York • Atlanta • Brussels • Chicago • Mexico City
San Francisco • Shanghai • Tokyo • Toronto • Washington, D.C.

Bulk discounts available. For details visit:
www.amacombooks.org/go/specialsales
Or contact special sales:
Phone: 800-250-5308
Email: specialsls@amanet.org
View all the AMACOM titles at: www.amacombooks.org
American Management Association: www.amanet.org

This publication is designed to provide accurate and authoritative information in regard to the subject matter covered. It is sold with the understanding that the publisher is not engaged in rendering legal, accounting, or other professional service. If legal advice or other expert assistance is required, the services of a competent professional person should be sought.

Library of Congress Cataloging-in-Publication Data

Steinberg, Abigail.
Recipe for success : an insider's guide to bringing your natural
food to market / Abigail Steinberg.
pages cm
Includes index.
ISBN 978-0-8144-3686-8 (pbk.) — ISBN 978-0-8144-3687-5 (ebook)
1. Natural foods industry. 2. Marketing. 3. Success in business. I. Title.
HD9000.5.S684 2015
641.3'020688—dc23
2015025461

About AMA

American Management Association (www.amanet.org) is a world leader in talent development, advancing the skills of individuals to drive business success. Our mission is to support the goals of individuals and organizations through a complete range of products and services, including classroom and virtual seminars, webcasts, webinars, podcasts, conferences, corporate and government solutions, business books, and research. AMA's approach to improving performance combines experiential learning—learning through doing—with opportunities for ongoing professional growth at every step of one's career journey.

Printing number
10 9 8 7 6 5 4 3 2 1

*In loving memory
of my stepfather, Hendrik Burgers,
whose guidance and unwavering strength
both as a businessman and as a human being
have been a source of inspiration
not only for this book, but for me
as a businesswoman.*

CONTENTS

FOREWORD

A prize-winning barbecue sauce. Your grandmother's recipe for. . . . Perhaps successful sales at San Diego's Hillcrest
and Little Italy Farmers markets hinting that a hobby can be
turned into a moneymaker. You know that Whole Foods Market has renovated its La Jolla store and opened a big new store
in Del Mar catering to the ever-increasing demand for natural
food products.

So maybe you are thinking it is time for you to get serious
about your natural food product. If you are, then it's time to
listen to Abigail Steinberg talk about "how to."

I have read business books. I have taught thousands of stu-
dents using business textbooks. I have even written business

books. I know that learning from a book is doable. But learning how to do something from most books is more of an iffy proposition.

Learning how to do something is like drilling down, layer by layer, into increasingly specific detail. It's that depth of hard-won experience that Steinberg brings to the reader. As you will read, many people already in the natural foods industry don't know what a turnover is, and how to do one correctly with Whole Foods Market or Sprouts Farmers Market. Get it wrong and your product never leaves their warehouses. Listen to Steinberg and get it right.

Starting with that first walk through a store, through product development and finding a distribution partner to the decision to expand or sell out, readers will find clear, specific guidance about how to deal with the many pitfalls and barriers included in *Recipe for Success* that they will encounter. Readers will also realize that the natural foods industry is not user-friendly, having more than its fair share of sharks, scoundrels, and store owners who are not interested in giving a neophyte a fair chance.

So, like any good how-to teacher, she shows you how to learn from her mistakes rather than your own.

David M. Hunter, B.A., M.B.A
Retired business professor (Brock University)
and author of *Supervisory Management*
and *Survival Guide to Business*

ACKNOWLEDGMENTS

Originally I felt writing acknowledgments would be a daunting task. But soon I realized it was finally a chance to thank all those who have supported me on this journey.

First off, I would like to thank my mother, Helen Burgers. It goes without saying I would not be here without her. But I also want her to know I appreciate the support and sacrifice she has made over the years. You have inspired me as a writer. You are also the most poised public speaker I have ever seen.

A very special thank you to my Grandma in England, Jeannette Livingstone. She has always been my biggest fan. Her unwavering support for my artistic endeavors is unmatched! She has never for a moment doubted me. I will forever appreciate her love, support, and like-minded artist soul.

To my dear husband Adam Edwards who has been my rock and support. I could not have written this book without you.

Thank you Dave Hunter for your mentorship. You kept me sane in this wonderful process.

Big thank you to my editor, Stephen S. Power, who believed in the book right from the start.

To my wonderful agent Albert Zuckerman who made it happen, fast! There is no way I could have done it without you.

I also want to thank all the people in my life. These are my family and friends behind the scenes. You are the people who made me who I am today. You all know who you are and what you have contributed on my life journey. So with that in alphabetical order I thank you!

Allison Claire-Acker, Silvia Aguila, Chi Chi (Yang) & Joe Bolton, Pearl Brook, Annemarie Brown-Mrmack and family, Cameron & Crystal Brown and children, Hugh & Marianne Brown, Edward & Barbara Burgers, Henk & Helen Burgers, Paul Burgers, Chi Chi (Yang), Bonnie Chermak, Sherryl Cowden, Adam Edwards, Gordon & Trish Edwards, Adam Forman, Jennifer Hempel. Bob Henderson, Robert & Carolyn Henderson, Diessa Henderson, Graham & Alexa Harris and children, Graham Harris, Geoffrey Harris, Louis & Adrienne Harris, Martin & Sheryl Harris, Shelley & Cory and Suzanne Hatt, Jim & Nicole and Sarah Hepworth, Rhonda and Brandon Hodges, Dave & Deana Hunter, Alana Jaq and family, Gina Juliano, Robert Knoll, Jay Krishan, Susan Laufer, Shelley Lavigne, Tara Law, Linda & Martin Lee, Lisa Linares, Charles & Jeannette Livingstone, Eric & Kate Marinho, Charmaine & Mark Mattison, Chloe Mattison, Abigail & Simon Mattison, Cameron McGlinchey, Deane McGlinchey, Edwardo Merlo, Jessica Mills, Kevin Mills, Jason & Gabby and Backy Nardell, Philip (not a problem!) Nardell, Michelle Nardell, Lisa & Kate and Wayne Parker, Evert Pater, Lais Pedroso, Stephen S. Power, Panda & Precious, Jordana Reim, Catherine Saul, Carol & David Steinberg, Joseph & Pearl Steinberg, Christina Kostoff & Jon Steinberg, Moe & Sybil Steinberg, Sharon Steinberg, Tana Steinberg, Linda Swanston, Neev Tapiero, Koya Webb, Michael Wadham, and my sweet nephews and soulmates Anthony & Patrick Wadham.

RECIPE
FOR
SUCCESS

1

YOUR FIRST STEP

You have the greatest new natural product, and it is sure to be a smash success! Your friends can't stop talking about it, so grocery stores across the country will never know what hit them, right? Before you risk thousands of dollars, though, bringing your product to market, keep reading. With this book I will show you how to navigate common problems, emotional pitfalls, and highly expensive traps that start-ups fall into and remain in on the path to success.

I have seen firsthand the many mistakes natural foods manufacturers make when trying to get their new product onto store shelves, costing themselves millions of dollars. For example, launching a product so similar to competitors' products that customers cannot tell the difference. Changing Universal Product Codes (UPCs) midlaunch and losing every account the company worked so hard to gain. Pushing a product that did not sell, slowly bankrupting the manufacturer. I don't want you to suffer the same self-inflicted wounds.

Others will try to wound you themselves. Buyers, stores, employees, distributors, brokers, and brand ambassadors all love new products, and surprisingly that is true even when a new product fails. Why? Because all of these players skim cash from your product. You will be encouraged to spend an exorbitant amount of cash on slotting fees, ads, MCB (Merchant Charge Back) and OI (Off Invoice), distributor setups, free-fills, brokers, demos, marketing, promotions, trade shows, table tops, mail outs, samples, and much more without actually increasing your sales. And even if you do, these players couldn't care less if you didn't see a penny yourself. I want you to, though.

The first few times that I encountered these mistakes, I thought, "This can't be normal." But when I saw them over and over again it left me wondering why new product manufacturers kept making them. In my search for an answer I discovered that there is not a single field guide to entering this trillion-dollar industry and traveling safely through its labyrinthine distribution channels. True, plenty of general business books exist. They explain strategy and global expansion, describe retailing and distributing, and discuss budgets and time management. They show you how to run a business in general, but not how to run a business in any specific industry. This book, however, gives you the secrets to running a natural foods business, including the following:

* ❖ Determining which retailers to target

* ❖ Finding distributors

* ❖ Finding brokers you can trust

* ❖ Developing an advertising and marketing plan

* ❖ Crafting an exit strategy

Who am I to write this book?

I am not perfect, of course. I have made mistakes. Better you learn from mine, though, instead of your own. If you can see your product on the shelf, then so can I, and if you have a dream, then let's dream big. Why not? Many have entered the natural products arena and come out as millionaires, whether they sold out to a competitor or secured venture capital money and became major players themselves.

For example, let me share a great story of the success of an Armenian man with a dream about tea. This man is Arsen Avakian. He saw just how successful and exciting Starbucks is for coffee lovers. In 2003, Arsen and his childhood friends created Argo Tea and set out to be the Starbucks of tea. Argo now has more than forty cafés. They have also taken their café success into the retail world. Their loose leaf teas and ready-to-drink (RTD) teas are in more than 14,000 retail locations, have generated more than $10 million in sales, and have created jobs for more than 500 employees. Kroger did call! All from dreaming big. Really big!

How did Arsen and his childhood buddies become the Starbucks of tea? One way was by turning a negative into a positive. In the face of a real estate recession Argo chose to expand and picked up several café locations in New York and Chicago. They import the best teas from around the world and create their own food and merchandise. In fact, everything in Argo cafés is Argo created. Not only do they want the finest teas from around the world but also the finest ingredients to make quality food for all types of diets. Word traveled fast, and in 2011 the *San Francisco Chronicle* hailed Argo as the company that would cause the twenty-first-century tea café revolution and get America to drink tea. *Time* magazine ran a story that agreed. In 2012, Argo decided to launch their RTD line of their best-selling cold teas because the demand was undeniable. Now Argo is in Kroger, Whole Foods Market, Sprouts Farmers Market, Walgreens, 7-Eleven, Ralphs, vending machines, hospitals, universities, and all the top distributors.

The natural products, supplements, and food industry is

important because it can change the way we eat, clean, and consume for the better. So don't treat this book as just a field guide or pocket reference for your success. Treat it as your means to change the world.

First, however, you have to get out of the kitchen and into the stores. It's time to take your first step.

2

BRINGING YOUR
FOOD TO MARKET

I t's not just your product that has to get out of the kitchen
and into the stores. It's you.

As you think about your new product, let's look at the
case of Michael, whose product, Michael's Perfect Pickles,
we'll come back to throughout this book. He sits at his kitchen
table staring at a bottle of his pickles. Michael's Perfect Pickles.
They are fine pickles. His family likes them, his friends like
them, and he received some great compliments about them at a
local flea market. But how can he find a real market for them?
What does it take, he wonders, to get them on the supermarket shelf? Why shouldn't someone buy his pickles instead of
someone else's?

The trouble is, Michael shops for groceries just like everyone else, but he has never actually seen the pickle aisle for what it is, a bewildering mixture of competing products. So before he can get his pickles on a supermarket shelf, he has to become an expert on that shelf. And that's what you have to do—become an expert on your product's shelf.

So how do you become an expert? Simple. Start with research, and the best research is hands-on. Go to a grocery store and purchase one or two successful items in your product category and figure out what makes them pop. Look at your competition. Snap a quick photo of the shelf and category you wish to be in. Find the average price point at desired retailers. And engage store personnel, who will be flattered to be asked for their opinions. Here are some questions you might ask:

❖ What products sell the most?

❖ Why do you think that is happening?

❖ What categories are most popular?

❖ What items do customers say they would never buy?

❖ What about traffic patterns? What days are heaviest? (The answers will help you determine the best times for demos.)

Once you know what the aisle is like and once you've started to think like a manufacturer instead of a consumer, you can begin to figure out how your product will fit in—or if it won't. There's no shame in admitting that. After all, the worst mistake you can make is trying to sell a product that clearly no one wants. Don't listen to your ego. Listen to the cash register.

SHELF CHECK ❖ 1

Know Thy Market

Observe your market carefully and ask yourself these seven questions:

1. Who's my target market?

2. How innovative does my product need to be?

3. What sets my product apart from the competition's?

4. Does my product have a look that is similar to the competition's?

5. What's the best price point for my category?

6. Is my category growing or shrinking?

7. Is my product in demand?

Who's My Target Market?

Store customers, buyers, distributors, retailers—they all want to know who your target market is, and they want you to be specific. Claiming that your product is for everyone *will not work*.

For example, if you are launching a natural antacid medicine, don't say it's for people ages eighteen to sixty-five. Most people with antacid problems are over thirty years old. This does not mean younger people won't need it too, but the thirty-plus category is your target. Let your marketing strategy follow suit.

How Innovative Does My Product Need to Be?

Simply replicating a competitor's product will not pay off because the market wants innovation and new products.

For example, I worked from just about day one with a natural soda company I'll call Z. Its mission was to launch a healthy soda without all the chemicals. At the start, the juggernaut competitor was obvious: Diet Coke. Now, this may seem like impossible competition. But it is not if you ask the correct question. Why was Diet Coke so popular? People wanted a Coca-Cola taste without calories or weight gain. Easy sell! Z capitalized on that market gap. It promoted stevia, the sweetener, so it could say that Z had no phosphoric acid or artificial ingredients. Z's pitch? A healthy soda without calories or artificial sweeteners. Z dominated the category because the company pioneered its category.

What Sets My Product Apart from the Competition's?

What sets your product apart? Perhaps it's the taste, quality, ingredients, environmental impact, or safety. Your sales angle should be defined by the most significant difference your product has. For example, one of my favorites is the only nontoxic cleaner on the market. Not only does it clean better than the alternatives on the stores' shelves, but if by chance your toddler finds it and drinks it down, it's 100 percent safe! Now, that's an angle everyone can appreciate. Thirty years ago, this product would have been science fiction. What a game changer! What about your product changes the game on its shelf?

I predict that edible cleaners will be a growing subcategory. Think about it: safe, edible cleaning products with no negative press about fires, poisoning, burns, or skin irritations. If you are considering manufacturing edible cleaning products, I believe this category to be wide open with few major players in the next few years. Jump into this category now and I may be talking about you in my next book.

It is very important to remind yourself that your competition has already spent millions to get to where they are today.

If you think you can launch a product as successful as Gatorade or Red Bull, by all means go for it. But to outspend these giants out of the gate while still an unproven brand will be risky. Battles can be short, but wars are notoriously long. To slay giants, your brand must raise the bar and differentiate itself.

Again, don't listen to your ego. I have worked with companies whose owners assumed their products were innovative. These were not realistic assumptions based on market research but unquestioned assumptions that led to amateurish packaging, less-flavorful products, and higher price points, all of which then resulted in a lack of sales. Once I suggested to a company that we rethink the launch of a new product because I thought we would be swallowed up by our competitors. The manufacturer's ego demanded otherwise, and a million dollars later the product moved from the shelves to the half-off bin and, from there, into obscurity.

Does My Product Have a Look That Is Similar to the Competition's?

This can and does happen. Inside supermarkets, when two products look similar, one must go because obtaining merchandise variety is important to retailers, except perhaps in a hyperspecialty store focusing on few categories.

I worked with a manufacturer whose packaging looked similar to its direct competition's, even down to the color scheme. The manufacturer did not imitate the competition—it was just unaware of them entirely. When its product eventually made it onto the shelf, even buyers and retailers thought they were the same brand. Worse, both products were placed together to reinforce the competitor's brand. I believe to this day that my manufacturer had a superior product. But the competitor had a larger stake in the market and a loyal following and methodically drove out its similarly packaged competitor.

What's the Best Price Point for My Category?

To answer this question you must first find your competitors' price points. You must humbly look at the competing products and their prices and ask if your price point should be the same or lower. This is another place where ego and good research can collide. *Cash flow is a fundamental of finance and must be a singular priority.* That may sound elementary, but if your cash dries up because of a poor pricing decision, you are in trouble. The majority of consumers compare pricing among brands, myself included. Aggressive price points can be instant sales killers. If you are going to charge a higher price there has to be a very clear reason or nobody will buy.

Products slightly cheaper than the next can instinctively draw a consumer's attention, whereas something overpriced will turn people off. An example would be a dish soap priced a dollar more than the competitive products. It is not a decadent piece of rare chocolate; it is a product for cleaning spoons.

Therefore, the consumer's tolerance for a higher price point is not as strong as for other, more-coveted items.

Having decided on your basic price you may find that you are not finished with pricing. Discounted sales provide another stream of revenue in the evolving grocery world. I have been observing the 99 Cents Only Stores and can see that discounting prices is a useful tactic. Unlike yesteryear when off brands sold cheaply, it's now top organic and mainstream brand products that can be discounted. If your production and operation costs are low from the start, that opens the doors to more pricing opportunities. If the day comes when your top specialty product is in overstock, then selling to the 99 Cents Only Stores and overstock sites will be a feasible alternative. When this happens, because of your low costs, you will close the deal with a profit. Do not think this will weaken your brand because the big organic brands are in the 99 Cents Only Stores to stay.

Is My Category Growing or Shrinking?

Shelf space allocation is regularly manipulated by retailers to increase sales and profits, in part because of trends in the market. So you have to know whether your category is growing or shrinking.

For example, the energy shot market boomed in recent years, naturally attracting competitors by the droves. Now some buyers I've spoken to believe this market may be shrinking, with the potential for enormous market casualties. Yes, one could argue that a breakout product could reactivate the category, but perhaps people are less willing to buy a 2.5-ounce shot for $3 to $4. Perhaps the current economy is dictating fewer impulse items and more staple items. When unemployment is high and money is tight, buying 16 ounces of fresh juice for $3 to $4 instead of a tiny shot seems like a better bang for your buck.

The way I see it, there are trends and fads. Trends can last a long time but fads come and go. Shots are a fading fad, and only a few suppliers will survive in the major retailers. Check the 99-cent store and you will see all these shots arriving in droves. Go to Whole Foods Market (WFM) and watch the dust gather on the shots. If you are going to jump on a fad, make sure you are the first in, not the last copycat.

Is My Product in Demand?

Launching a product can be likened to bringing a child into the world. But be careful of the emotional commitment. You must ask if there is a real demand for your product. Retail buyers are already inundated with thousands of new and established products. Is your category saturated with products or is there room for one more? How can you get brand share?

Better yet, can you invent a new category? Can you make your product so innovative that it will be an undeniable hit? For example, the company called Ezekiel came out with sprouted wheat shells and breads. When Ezekiel launched these products they were all the rage because consumers wanted live sprouted bread with low carbs and, most important, healthier bread. Ezekiel came to dominate that space. Ezekiel became one of the top brand shares of the sprouted bread category. It was a paradigm shift.

Recently I visited my favorite WFM in Venice, California, looking for my Ezekiel shells and found none. Nothing caught my eye as similar and, irritated, I drove to Sprouts Farmers Market to buy them. Loyal customers will jump a few hurdles to buy a favorite product. It's one thing to create a product people will pay money for. It's another to create one that people will also pay for with time and effort.

So let's go on to the next step: moving your product from conception to retail ready.

LOCKED & LOADED

From Concept
to
Retail Ready

S o you are back from the stores with the knowledge gained from your research. Let's use it to get started on your big dream. We will do that in a simple way by looking at a typical store layout, as depicted in Figure 3-1.

You can see the location of departments such as produce, meat, seafood, dairy, baked goods, snacks, chips, and beverages. In the last decade or two, additional categories and specialty categories have been added, many of which are part of the natural foods industry. These include super fruit, dairy alternatives, functional juices, other functional beverages, shots, antioxidants, and probiotic beverages. Dozens and doz-

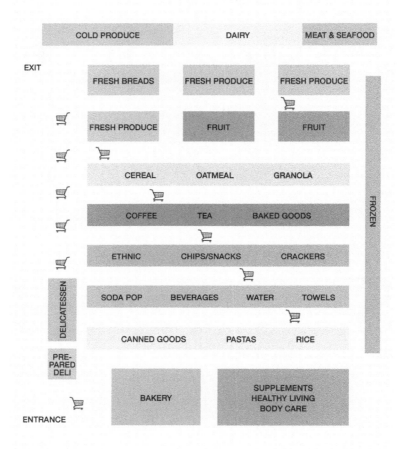

Figure 3-1. Where do you see your product?

ens of products line the shelves, and many of them look similar and do similar things. How do you make your product stand out?

You do that by thinking very carefully about packaging and what it costs. Your package is the face of your company and should include the images most crucial to representing you. Picking the correct packaging is like preparing for the most important meeting of your life, so it has to be right from start to finish or your meeting will fail. Now, to give you an idea of what you need to do to get ready, let's use the example of Michael's Perfect Pickles. Michael decides on a clear jar to display his organic dills. Clear jars are most popular for pickles and they look cool too (see Figure 3-2).

A rgo Tea provides one example of smart and sustainable packaging. Argo Tea knew that creating an RTD tea in thick glass bottles would be more expensive than using aluminum cans. However, the glass bottles not only look cool, they keep the product tasting great and are reusable, sustainable, recyclable, and attractive to customers. Argo Tea now purchases glass bottles in such mass quantities that their cost has become much lower. In turn, Argo Tea products are affordable and at the perfect price point for their category. At the beginning of 2015, Argo Tea had more than $10 million in sales and projects sales in excess of $12 million for 2016.

As Michael envisioned his package design, he needed to remember that it is not just about what customers will see on the shelf. It is also about what will be seen when he promotes his product in print, on the Internet, in a point-of-purchase display, or on television. Your design work will be helped by more research: talking to a local printer, meeting with your teenage cousin who designs websites, having a chat with a sales rep of a newspaper where you live, and so forth.

You want to make the right decisions for your key retailers. For example, many natural and premium retailers are shying away from canned products because of the risk of BPA (bisphenol A) and are looking at glass alternatives. Premium retailers are also shy about aluminum-packaged products, because aluminum has been connected with Alzheimer's disease. Existing aluminum products on the shelf might have been "grandfathered in," but there is a good chance that consumers will demand a change, retailers will change ingredient and packaging policies, or both. You would be surprised how many products have had to have their packaging changed in response to these types of requests. Perhaps as a consumer you've seen soda brands change from a can to a bottle. This is most likely a result of a request by buyers and a changing market. Make sure you research your key retailers to ensure that you don't use materials and ingredients they have banned or are shying away from. If you start right you won't have to change down the road when it costs you a lot more to do so.

The Food and Drug Administration's (FDA) website, www.fda.gov, is a great resource center for industry information. There is a tab called Recalls that you can use to research all the recalls from past to present. The recall information lists products, stores, and reasons for recalls. This site can be a handy tool to look up competitors' recalls or simply to see what can go wrong, especially if a product similar to yours was recalled.

Lock Your Package and Product Before Printing and FDA Approval

After you create your package and get FDA approval, make sure you lock it down because any change later will cost money and time.

The container will need to have a label that answers consumers' questions as well as meeting the demands of packaging regulations. Your product's most important attributes should be listed in plain sight. For example, words like *organic, low fat, sugar free, low sodium, dairy free*, and *low carbs* are eye-catching. However, note that you can't claim to consumers, retailers, or buyers that your product is organic, kosher, or non–genetically modified organism (non-GMO) without certification.

Certifications are extremely important in the natural foods world. Natural market consumers will pick up products with kosher, non-GMO, and certified organic certifications because of their chosen lifestyle.

Of all certifications the following are the most important.

USDA Organic

In many way this is one of the most important of the certifications. Why? Think about it. When someone gives you a "certified organic" product, what's the first thing that comes to your mind? This is a healthy, quality product. I feel safe eating this organic food. I feel safe washing my hair with this organic shampoo. I know that from farm to table the farmers, ranchers, and processors of this product have followed rigorous U.S. Department of Agriculture (USDA) standards, including what can be added and how any animals have been treated.

What does this sense of security equate to? Sales!

WEBSITE: WWW.USDA.GOV

NON-GMO

As stated previously, GMO means genetically modified organism. When a product is certified non-GMO it means that it was not created by scientists genetically modifying a variety of the product. There is a lot of food out there that is GMO. Now you must wonder why one would genetically modify food. Genetic modification started when scientists were searching for a way for plants to resist certain pesticides and herbicides. For example, when farmers spray their genetically modified corn most of the pests will be destroyed without affecting the corn.

GMO crops can grow larger because they can fight pests. In some cases, farmers can actually use a more environmentally friendly crop spray and less of it too. This all sounds great, right? Sounds good but there is a downside.

Pests will become resistant to the sprays, and then spraying crops will become useless. When GMO plants pollinate nearby similar crops, they transfer the modified genes, which ultimately transfer to humans and animals. GMO is often found in corn, soya beans, and sugarcane. This is why natural and organic foods stores will often require organic and non-GMO corn, soya beans, and cane sugar. Natural and organic foods stores hold themselves to a higher standard to meet their customer demands for certified non-GMO foods.

The Non-GMO Project is a nonprofit organization that works to preserve and build the non-GMO food supply. What it does is educate consumers and provide verified non-GMO choices. Its members believe that everyone should have an informed choice to consume or not consume genetically modified organisms.

The Non-GMO Project is governed by a board of directors who collectively decide whether a product meets the required certification. They are a collaborative network of technical and communications advisers from all backgrounds and sectors.

WEBSITE: WWW.NONGMOPROJECT.ORG

Kosher

Kosher is another certification that will open your product to a multitude of opportunities in the kosher marketplace. Kosher practices govern the types of food that an observant Jewish person may eat and the ways in which they may be prepared. To be certified kosher, all ingredients in every product—and the process of preparing the product—must be certified for kosher compliance too. This means demanding inspections but it's worth it.

WEBSITE: WWW.OK.ORG

These certifications will be important in many markets, and often certification is the deciding factor for acceptance, rejection, buy, or not buy. Some markets don't take any products without certification. In fact, certification is becoming increasingly imperative. If any of these certifications relate to your product, get them. It's worth it.

Once you have your certifications in place and your packaging is set, don't change them. However, if you must, I recommend waiting a minimum of a year or two after consistent placement on retail shelves. You want to establish a loyal and identifiable consumer following. So evolve before launch. Take time to create what you want and to be confident in your packaging before you send it off to be reviewed by your accounts.

Distributors and retailers will request product images for all setup and ad deals. If you change packaging after launch, old images will be published in all ads and books. Once published, distributor books and ads cannot be changed for at least three months.

Retailers' ads have similar restrictions for making changes after their publication deadlines. And *all* changes will require much correspondence, time, and, above all, money. Packaging and promotion changes in the first year of launch are an unnecessary way to lose money and time right out of the gate. It's best to take an extra month or two for final decisions rather than twice as much time and needed operating cash for clearing changes after launch.

Once your product formulation is locked, your packaging is complete, and the FDA confirms that you will not harm anyone with your product (or at least your package has the required warnings), the next step is to acquire a Universal Product Code (UPC), although you can also apply during your product and package design process.

The UPC is the bar code commonly found on the side, bottom, or top of a product. It is what stores scan at registers and use to process deliveries and various orders. It's also the code that distributors refer to when selling your product. When retailers order product, they do not do so just by name. They will use the UPC, or an assigned distributor coding. I refer to item numbers (or distributor coding) in Chapter 4.

The only company you should use to obtain your UPCs is GS1, found on the Internet at www.gs1us.org. GS1 is the standard compliant UPC that is recognized at major retailers across the globe. It is a nonprofit international organization that develops and maintains standards for supply-and-demand chains across multiple sectors. UPCs come in batches of 10 sequential codes, each referred to as a family of UPCs. This is the industry standard of UPCs. When someone says, "Are you GS1 compliant?" you should be able to say, "Yes!"

Do Not, Under Any Circumstances, Change Your UPC

I'll put it simply: If you change your UPC at any time, you will kill your product.

I worked for a company I'll refer to as Lemon-Lime. It launched four stock keeping units (SKUs). All four were accepted by 500 retailers such as Lassens Natural Foods & Vitamins, Clark's Nutrition & Natural Foods Market, and distributors such as UNFI (United Natural Foods, Inc.), KeHE, and Nature's Best. Lemon-Lime decided, within a few months after placement, to change its aluminum cans to plastic bottles. This was a massive undertaking. And, hitting everyone involved like a tornado, it simultaneously adjusted artwork and altered product names! The bottles looked nothing like the old product's packages, and the SKUs had changed. Neither consumers nor retailers could recognize them as the same brand.

Dozens of demos, ads, and other marketing activities promised to land the accounts in the first place were performed with old packaging. What a waste! We needed to change the names and packaging information with all the distributors. The sales director was caught in an avalanche of administrative work. It took days to fill out distributor paperwork with questions asking everything imaginable—from weight, height, tie-downs (i.e., pallet dimensions), pallet sizes, product images, insurance, UPCs, packaging details, sourcing, and shipping, all the way down to ingredient breakdowns—from our co-packers. In a small start-up, this meant two to three weeks of wasted labor, resources, and capital.

Don't think you can slip a change by anyone either. Retailers and distributors will notice if you switch in an altered product and don't communicate. Your shipment will be rejected as not matching the original specifications. You will be hit with shipment/return costs and the likelihood of your product being placed on hold. Old product will be listed as out of stock or, worse, discontinued. When a retailer attempts to buy your product, there will not be an explanation.

The results for Lemon-Lime were months of nonsales, sabotaged product deliveries, and choked cash flow. The worst part? This was self-induced.

To change packaging officially, the company had to recall the product and replace it with new product at all retailer and distributor locations. Unfortunately, retailers did not appreciate the change because it confused customers. I remember the frustrations that just seemed to multiply. Lemon-Lime had even changed the UPC on one of the new bottles. The company ran out of the family of UPCs because it had another product line in a similar category and shared it with the new one. Then the company realized it had to buy another family of UPCs, so another family was purchased and thrown into the mix. It really does not matter what your reason is for wanting to change a UPC—don't do it.

Total Recall:
Sometimes Bad Things Happen

If you contract out work you will still be responsible for its quality. So you must continually assess the quality of your contractors' work. You might have a co-packer that is bottling your product. Let me define a co-packer. A co-packer is a company that manufactures and packages foods or other products for its clients. A co-packer will be absolutely necessary unless you want to run a factory to manufacture your product. More often than not entrepreneurs need to pass the ball to a co-packer. However, you end up paying if you don't catch the co-packer's mistakes.

I worked with a company that had a fine beverage but, unbeknownst to them, their co-packer changed their lids ever so slightly. The change wasn't even visible to the naked eye. Nonetheless, it was enough to let air get into the bottles. The result: mold and leaking. And worse, the mold and leaking were just in one or two bottles in every tenth or eleventh case. It took numerous complaints and a loss of sales and retailers to get to the bottom of the problem.

As is ever too common in this industry, this beverage company was aware of the problem for over six months. When their junior management became aware of the issue and let superiors know, they still refused to pull existing product. The rationale? Overstocked. They waited until every single moldy, leaky bottle sold. This was out of my decision-making control and was demeaning to the reputable company I represented. The biggest sin of this beverage company is that they were lying to customers, distributors, and retailers. In fact, McLane had a total recall on this beverage just before the big 7-Eleven show. The whole thing was, to say the least, embarrassing.

So what do you do when a crisis happens? Find out which companies have received bad product and put your best PR hat on. Visit every affected account, replace the product, and assure them you are there for them. Chances are retailers will stick with you if you have a good product. They just want to be heard. They want to know you will be there if there is a problem. The result? You will retain all your customers and keep going. Almost every manufacturer at one time or another experiences a problem. The key is how you respond. A company is not judged just by the actual problem it has but also by how it resolves it. So if this happens to you, take a breath and deal with it one retailer at a time.

I was faced with cleaning up the moldy situation. It had some retailers and distributors on their heels. If you move as slow as molasses in January you will lose accounts, distributors, and industry respect. So our team of brand ambassadors and merchandisers went to every retailer and replaced the moldy product with fresh product within forty-eight hours of the complaint. The result: no business lost. In fact, we made stronger ties, thanks to the shared adversity.

However, it took another four months for this mold problem to completely disappear. I was putting out fires every step of the way. The manufacturing problem needed to be repaired, but, unfortunately, production is often about three to four months ahead of actual store delivery to ensure that product is available in distributors' warehouses. I had inspectors go to every distributor warehouse to remove any compromised product. As annoying and time-consuming as it was, it just had to be done. When retailers or distributors witness a manufacturer faced with that kind of adversity cleaning up a mess as gracefully as a samurai, they give respect. These retailers or distributors have your team's direct contact numbers in case anything goes wrong again in the future. To retailers, that level of comfort is priceless.

SHELF CHECK ❖ 4

Initially Launch Three to Five SKUs

A modern and complex consumer-centric landscape almost demands that you and your team launch multiple SKUs from the beginning. Most manufacturers launch a minimum of three to five SKUs. This aids a new brand in becoming immediately visible. In the case of Michael launching Michael's Perfect Pickles, one lone pickle jar on the shelf won't cut it, but three taste variations of the original would be smart.

Now Michael has four products manufactured and four potential SKU placements. Time to start developing a few more SKUs. Pay attention to sales trends. If one SKU is not performing, consider dropping it. Upon the next retail category review, you can present your new item, which shows you to be a nimble, adaptable, and smart vendor.

SHELF CHECK ❖ 5

Remember: New Items = ATTENTION

Note: I am not advocating accelerated growth early on. Three to five SKUs is a conservative, modest start. The reason I suggest this number is that one SKU will get lost in a sea of other products, but three to five SKUs pop on the shelves. And let's face it: Not every SKU will be a hit. Sometimes you launch five SKUs and one of them just does not sell as well. Or in some markets they want only the top one or two. I worked with a company that had to discontinue one of its SKUs because it just was not selling enough. However, with customer feedback it invented another SKU to replace it. The company found later that everyone was replacing this one failed SKU with this breakout hit. The result: same shelf space, more sales.

Fortunately, most start-ups can achieve a feel for the market with a launch of three to five SKUs, in part because new items bring energy and excitement to retailers and distributors and, most important, to customers.

Obviously the number depends on the category. There are dozens of spices and herbs used in cooking, so to get noticed a spice manufacturer would want to launch with a larger than normal number of SKUs, perhaps ten to fifteen. One of the positive aspects of items like spices is that they don't weigh much. This means direct sales and shipping will be relatively inexpensive. Beverages, on the other hand, are heavy and expensive to ship, and a large number of initial SKUs would be too costly.

One way to hit the market at a perfect time is to offer holiday SKUs. This can be very lucrative although competitive. There are popular trade shows with KeHE and UNFI completely dedicated to holiday SKUs. If you can get the holiday hit it can boost sales in magical ways. An example is the vegan line Gardein. It launched a vegan product called Stuffed Turk'y. This limited-edition holiday SKU is available around Thanksgiving and Christmas and becomes one of the most popular SKUs. We all wait anxiously until the holidays to buy Stuffed Turk'y. I often buy this at Target. Yes, Target! Gardein has not only hit the big time in the natural foods industry with this SKU but crossed over to the mainstream.

MorningStar Farms is another delightful vegetarian company. Their Grillers Prime has turned the veggie burger into burgers that can fool any meat eater. To date, at every barbeque I have thrown I have had meat eaters demanding the Grillers Prime vegetarian burgers. This item is such a hit it is often sold out or close to it at retailers, so I usually need to buy the jumbo box to ensure a supply.

Companies like Gardein and MorningStar Farms have their own section at Target. Ten years ago it would not have been possible to support such a section in Target. Now, not only is it possible to have meatless options at Target, it's very profitable. How great is that for the natural foods industry!

4

DISTRIBUTORS

A
Necessary
Partnership

D istributors are expensive, demanding, and absolutely essential. Retailers can't buy directly from the hundreds of manufacturers of the thousands of products they have in their stores. So buyers at retail chains typically purchase from one or two preferred distributors to service their stores. That way a huge variety of product arrives at each store packed neatly on pallets with a single invoice to be paid for all the different products. Top distributors will also supply retailers with a blanket discount, special deals, preferred service from reps, and lavish treatment at distributor trade shows. These buyers may turn to minor distributors and direct sales in order to fill gaps on their stores' shelves, but you want to be with the preferred distributors that stores already work with. Just as distributors make things convenient and efficient for buyers, they can incorporate your product into an existing order on a Nature's Best, UNFI, or KeHE delivery truck, making things convenient and efficient for you too.

What Does a Distributor Do?

Distributors are the veins in the body of the retail industry. Distributors buy in bulk from suppliers like you. They then "break" the bulk shipments into smaller quantities and store them at their distribution centers. When an order arrives from a retail account, the various items needed to fill the order are pulled together. A truck is loaded up and the order is delivered to the account. They are, essentially, supermarkets for supermarkets.

Getting into a distributor is not easy, and as you will read, they do have a number of requirements. But if you can meet them you are in the club. It's a club you must be part of to some degree to be successful in the natural foods industry.

Distributors: Easy or Tough?

Distributors can be pretty tough because they know what it's like to be burned. For instance, one company expanded its business from Canada to the United States. It was in every distributor. Nonetheless, for many reasons the company went bankrupt. All its distributors were left with product nobody was ordering. Ultimately, distributors had to sell off product at deep discounts or eat the costs of expiring product. This is not an uncommon situation. As a result, new vendors with little or no experience are often seen as unreliable. But remember, experience and sales open doors fast!

Before a distributor will purchase pallets of an unproven product, the distributor will want to see real demand. Warehouse space is valuable, and unproven products are given very little shelf space. Don't expect any distributor to buy in high quantities unless customers are demanding your product.

That said, distributors are your partners. They want your product to sell for the same reason you do: profit. If you coordinate with them properly, they will serve you and your brand well. Depending on how aggressive you and/or your sales directors are, you can use them to close major deals.

What Distributors Require

* ❖ Commitments and preorders from at least eight to ten of their customers.

* ❖ Properly completed paperwork. Most packages require twenty-plus pages to be filled out.

* ❖ Liability insurance to cover any damaged or destroyed

product. Each distributor has specific insurance require-ments. Meet them.

❖ A 15 percent discount for the first three months on intro-ductory items.

❖ Yearly promotions such as 15 percent discounts during your peak sales months. For example, for a dietary sup-plement, January (New Year's resolution month) and/or summer bikini time would be a good promotional focus!

❖ Guaranteed product. If product is expired or damaged, you take it back. Be sure about this and *do not* send soon-to-be-expired product.

❖ Formulations. Your suppliers will have your formulations or products they have supplied to you. To define formu-lation, it's your recipe broken down into detailed ingre-dients. It is not as simple as giving your recipe because once you get into consumer goods it's beyond the recipe. Formulations comprise nutritional breakdowns, ingredient sources, and recipe. Sometimes where you source your ingredients may have a bearing on a buyer's decision, such as if your ingredient goes against a free trade policy. Ingredient specifics is something you would obtain from your co-packers because they can supply you the nutritional chart, ingredient breakdown, and ingredient sources. Sometimes it takes a few weeks to obtain formulations from your co-packers, so get them at the first opportunity.

❖ Product details such as pallet size, UPC, height, price, weight, suggested retail price (SRP), wholesale price, and every other minor detail imaginable. Creating price sheets for your team with all these details before approaching a distributor would be wise, as well as time-saving.

❖ Commitments to their trade shows for at least the first year.

❖ Adherence to protocols about schedule deliveries.

❖ Punctuality for product delivery appointments. Otherwise, you will be turned away.

SHELF CHECK ❖ 6

Know the Five Major Distributor Networks

The five dominant broadline distributors in the natural/specialty market are Nature's Best, UNFI, KeHE, Core-Mark, and McLane. Other major distributors exist, and these five can be costly at times, but they are your best bets for success. Broadline distributors are major distributors that deliver product to retailers with a markup of approximately 7 to 15 percent.

At their trade shows they can help you find the sales gold mines and extract the lucrative deals that will launch your product and jump-start your company. For example, at the 2012 KeHE summer selling show in Chicago, I connected with a KeHE sales rep in charge of the H-E-B markets at more than 150 stores. The rep responded positively to our product, taking samples and literature away with him. Periodically over the next six months I called and emailed this sales rep. I did not hear from him so I sent additional samples and kept that contact alive. A few months later? The KeHE sales rep informed me we had closed a major deal. A few weeks later the product was *in every H-E-B store.* The same KeHE rep closed a deal for us through his buyer connections. Now that's a good partner!

Let's look at the big five:

I have worked with companies that refuse to learn turnovers, the forms used to place orders with wholesalers. These turnovers are what you use to fax or email an order to Nature's Best and UNFI. When I left Lemon-Lime, the team had no idea what a Nature's Best or UNFI turnover was or how to fill one out. That level of ignorance is beyond excusable. Let that not be you.

Nature's Best

I love Nature's Best, the largest privately owned wholesaler-distributor of health and natural foods products in the natural products industry. They have many valuable accounts: Sprouts; Raley's; adored retailers such as Mother's Market & Kitchen; Lassens; Clark's; and hundreds of natural/specialty independent retailers. They are also the best distributor to start with. And although they use distribution centers in California and Texas, their distribution channels extend as far as Hawaii. The trade shows Nature's Best puts on have a comfier ambience than other distributors'. In addition, their sales teams are smaller but solid enough to remain powerfully influential and help accomplish your goals. In fact, a salesperson from Nature's Best works right inside the corporate office at Raley's approving items. (Wink, wink.) I highly recommend Nature's Best and their family-oriented lifestyle–like staff.

For salespeople it's easy to submit turnover orders to Nature's Best. You simply fill out the turnover and email or fax it in. Nature's Best supplies the turnover forms. Also, any broker worth anything will have these turnovers on hand.

They specialize in retail marketing support, Web services, business analysis tools, and sales/category management consulting.

In my opinion, Nature's Best is one of the easiest major distributors to work with. The reason is, it's like working with a family. As I said before, it's the most ideal distributor to start with. In my experience, they take the least amount of time to set products up with item numbers (i.e., distributor coding). Nature's Best will get the ball rolling for you. Then you can go to other major distributors after some success with Nature's Best. (In July 2014 Nature's Best was acquired by KeHE, but they still operate as two separate distributors.)

WEBSITE: WWW.NATURESBEST.NET

For a reasonable fee, Nature's Best will supply you with sales reports. I recommend this once you are off to the races and sales begin to pick up. They do require detailed paperwork, and acceptance is not guaranteed. But the value of their established connections is obvious.

Nature's Best is also accommodating if you need to pick up product from their warehouse for samples and demos. This is handy for smaller companies with no local warehouse space to store product. It also minimizes your shipping expenses. However, a pickup appointment is required.

I have consulted with companies that target Nature's Best from the beginning. In the real world, sometimes a simple phone call can accomplish this. For other items and considering category competition, a little coaxing and selling is necessary.

NOTE: Nature's Best uses a six-digit item code for each SKU of your product. From the day your codes are issued they will be your product codes for all retail accounts to order your product. These codes will never change, nor would you want them to. These are the codes that will be printed in Nature's Best sales books and promotions. Now, for a bit of enlightenment. Without an initial order, Nature's Best will wait to issue a PO (purchase order from retailers) until you have at least five or six POs. This means that without codes you need retailers to commit to bringing in your product. It's kind of like the chicken or the egg. You need the codes for orders but you also need orders to generate codes. So get commitments for orders when your product is ready and in stock.

Nature's Best has one-time setup fees for use of their sales team and for inclusion in the Nature's Best publication as well as additional fees for ads including color ad slicks. (Simply put, ad slicks are color ads that are loose within the buyer's publication.)

UNFI

UNFI is the leading independent national distributor of natural, organic, and specialty foods and related products, including nutritional supplements, personal care items, and organic produce, in the United States. They also distribute in Canada. UNFI has thousands of coveted accounts. These include

Meijer, WFM, Publix, Publix GreenWise Markets, Safeway, Bristol Farms, and Jimbo's . . . *Naturally!* as well as thousands of major service accounts.

WEBSITE: WWW.UNFI.COM

UNFI may be the most demanding of all distributors because of their administrative requirements. UNFI requires pre-sales because there is only so much space they can give to unproven products in their distribution centers. But trust me, it's worth the effort to meet this difficult requirement because the major retailers that draw only from UNFI distribution centers will be open to reviewing your product.

NOTE: It is important to be aware that UNFI generates two sets of five-digit item numbers (distributer codes). One set is for the West and one is for the East. And you are not allowed to sell product in one region using the other region's codes. Even your trade show attendance request must be coded for the correct region. If you are coded for the West only, guess what? You are not heading east, yet.

Don't count your free-range chickens before they're hatched; keep in mind that it can take up to a year to obtain codes. UNFI struggles with demand for warehouse space. Very few companies can stockpile inventory anymore—if any. So expect a six-month window to generate codes from UNFI for the west region and another six for the east. Be persistent.

Yes, you will need stellar sales numbers to forge a deal with the major retail accounts. Even if you don't have those numbers you can still forge relationships, but getting in requires proof of success. Remember, everyone wants in on the big retail accounts like WFM and Sprouts Farmers Market. You need to show that your products can go beyond mom-and-pop stores and be real players. Getting into the major distributors can launch a product fast!

UNFI hosts effective tabletop shows, most notably in Portland, Oregon; and Orlando, Florida. This pair of shows generates excellent attendance and creates unique opportunities. A real drawing card to these shows is the opportunity to schedule one-on-one meetings with UNFI sales representatives as well as the buyers of your target chains an entire day before show launch. In essence, you are speed dating your distributors. In a large noisy room you are allowed fifteen minutes for each meeting. At the end of that time a bell chimes and you are off to see another potential partner. So you can simultaneously make connections and be instantly educated about various distributors.

For salespeople UNFI is an easy company to submit turn-over orders to. You simply fill out the turnover and email or fax it in. UNFI supplies turnover forms, and any competent broker will have these turnovers on hand as well.

UNFI is the #1 distributor for WFM. When you con-nect with WFM start your UNFI paperwork imme-diately because it can take up to nine months to get approval and codes!

NOTE: UNFI has one-time setup fees for use of their sales team and for inclusion in the UNFI publication as well as additional fees for ads including color ad slicks.

KeHE

KeHE (which also owns Nature's Best, which they purchased in 2015) works with retailers at every level: national, regional, and all sizes of grocery chains and independent retailers. Their reach as a major distributor extends beyond the United States to Canada and all the way to South America.

WEBSITE: WWW.KEHE.COM

With 3,500 manufacturers, importers, and other product supply partners, there is virtually no limit to the assortment of products that KeHE makes available to their retailers. Their team could be out there selling your product every day, and you will see it in real time!

NOTE: KeHE codes by UPC. Unlike Nature's Best, Core-Mark, and UNFI, they *do not generate item codes.* This should reinforce any crazy notion of ever changing UPC codes. In fact, a KeHE rep once called changing a UPC "death to an item." KeHE has one-time setup fees for use of their sales team and for inclusion in the KeHE publication as well as additional fees for ads including color ad slicks.

KeHE has the best and most entertaining trade shows. I highly recommend their popular Summer Selling Show. Attendance is expensive. What makes it expensive? No, it's not the tickets. You will find yourself paying around $200 or more per day to stay at the hotel hosting the trade show, which saves you the hassle of driving back and forth to the show. Meals out can be around $20 to $60 per person. It will depend on whether you plan to wine-and-dine customers. You'll pay at least $5,000 to $7,000 for a five-by-ten booth. Sometimes you can opt to share a booth, which can be cost-effective. And you'll have shipping costs also. You will get at least two passes for your booth for you and a worker. I suggest you don't work it alone. Too much for one person. You never want to leave your booth empty—ever.

Despite the expense, fascinating opportunities are bountiful at trade shows. KeHE has a set process for reviewing new items before the show. Acceptance to these shows is not automatic. Send in all paperwork completed per instructions. Imagine your product in huge retail partners like H-E-B, Publix, Publix GreenWise Markets, Winn-Dixie, and so many more. These are the players who attend.

What I love about KeHE is that you can monitor all your sales, ads, and other details in real time on KeHE's online site called OAK. Who doesn't want to know their distribution center's stock levels in real time? Or if a PO has been issued? Or the quantities they sell to each retailer and which distribution center is most successful? The site is not easy to use, though, so I recommend that you have individuals who have worked with it on your team.

Core-Mark

Core-Mark is a mainstream broadline distributor. This means they service a lot of the mainstream accounts and C-stores (convenience stores). For example, if you feel your product would thrive in C-stores, universities, hospitals, gas stations, hotels, and restaurants, then you've hit the jackpot. Core-Mark covers all this and more.

Core-Mark has been around for more than 120 years! Since starting in 1888 as Glaser Bros. a single storefront in San Francisco, it has grown to be one of the largest distributors and marketers of consumer goods in North America.

Core-Mark has monthly open houses and sales meetings that are free to attend. I suggest your team attend every single one until your product is known within Core-Mark regions.

WEBSITE: WWW.CORE-MARK.COM

McLane

McLane is the biggest of the big, an international broadline distributor that covers 7-Eleven, gas stations, convenience stores, hotels, hospitals, and universities. To put things in perspective, if WFM takes your product, they can put it in nearly 400 stores. If McLane gets your product into gas stations, it could be in thousands of outlets. McLane, along with Core-Mark, defines the mainstream.

McLane prides itself on innovation, integrity, and leadership. It evolved from a distributor of the smaller retail grocer in 1894 to a leading grocery wholesaler and distributor in the 1960s and 1970s to a worldwide logistics powerhouse in the

1990s. Today, McLane is a supply chain services leader, delivering more than 10 billion pounds of merchandise to customers every year.

McLane hosts the 7-Eleven franchise shows. These shows are costly, meaning you could spend upward of $6,000 for a booth, but it's well worth it. You will need plenty of product and a way to get it there. I suggest you bring it to the show yourself—that is the easiest way. You will also need to stay at the hotel unless you live near the show location. You will need help at the booth, plus the time it takes to organize the show. Get into 7-Eleven and you are money! I have worked for a company that claims that 35 percent of its $12 million annually in sales is from McLane. If I did not see the thousands and thousands of dollars in orders daily, I would not believe it. The greatest part is, these are low-maintenance accounts, meaning no demos or constant store visits. It's an automatic order.

WEBSITE: WWW.MCLANECO.COM

SHELF CHECK ❖ 7

Use Your Distributor Sales Reps— They Are Working for You!

Distributors like Nature's Best, KeHE, Core-Mark, McLane, and UNFI sell their products using sales representatives in the field. These employees introduce and market new items for placement in their existing accounts. These distributor sales reps receive incentives and bonuses from their distributor (employer) and/or manufacturers like you as they secure accounts. Good reps have many long-standing relationships. Distribution partners can bring life to stagnant sales. It's a win-win situation for you.

As soon as I get a product into a distributor I start calling their sales reps. Who better to walk me into retail accounts that I have no relationship with? That's right. Be sure to get a list of your distributor's sales reps and their contact information when you are accepted by a distributor. Reps are paid to provide customer service and aid in advancing your brand. You need their support to ensure closing new business.

Utilize distributor sales reps, but don't expect that the minute you sign up with a distributor every rep will be begging for your attention. From their perspective, the inflow of new vendors is incessant, and they come and go with monotonous regularity. Nevertheless, cultivate the hired help.

So you ask, What should one expect to pay when joining a distributor? There are setup fees ranging from $500 to $5,000 depending on the distributor. These charges often come off your first invoice. These charges are associated with new item publications, distributor ads, distributor trade shows, new item programs, and free-fills for their sales reps. There are distributor trade shows you must commit to at least twice the first year, and you must commit to sell your product to as many of their customers as possible. Distributors are not cheap! But if you want in you must pay the entrance fees. Be specific about your needs and be clear.

> Just because your product is in major distributors does not mean you are guaranteed their accounts. There will always be negotiations and costs, and most of all patience is needed.

Connect with Your Distributor Account Buyers

Create a relationship with your distributor account buyers. Every distributor has account buyers for each category. For example, there are dairy buyers and health and body care buyers.

Distributor buyers are a superb resource. They can give you a list of distributor sales reps and their territories. They can swiftly push new items through for distribution approval. Develop a strong relationship with your buyer. If you create a product in another category, you can contact your regular account buyer to get a referral to the new account buyer you need to contact. They are also a great resource as you move around the natural foods industry. As in all industries, people are highly connected, and I consider that doubly so for the natural foods industry.

Prepare for the Trade Shows

All right, you are set up with KeHE, UNFI, Nature's Best, Core-Mark, or McLane and have signed up for all their trade shows. How do you prepare for them?

Make sure that every sales rep at your distributor knows you and your product. This advance marketing could take several months, during which you send out samples and sales sheets to every rep. After a period of time, though, you will start receiving sales reports from all over the nation, your efforts rewarded by the distributors. Priceless!

Customize your sales sheets. Both distributors and retailers love customized sheets because they make life so much easier for everyone! The minute you are *accepted by a distributor with item codes* create a customized sales sheet including images of the item(s); UPC(s); distributor item code(s); distributor logo; your company logo; your sales rep and/or sales director info; and, most important, ingredient lists. List ingredients or you will be asked what they are every time you show—to everyone's aggravation. Product ingredients are what natural foods are all about. Highlight them; don't hide them.

Get a list of retailers and hit them up! Get account lists from sales reps. Send them samples and sales sheets. Treat these samples and sales sheets as unique gift boxes. Personalize them when you can—be interesting and different, and cut through the noise. The more advance legwork you do, the easier it is for you and/or your broker/distributor to close accounts.

What I do is get a list of contacts from my distributor and send personalized emails to every single buyer. They say something like, "Your distributor sales rep thinks our product is a perfect fit because . . ." You may not get a response to every email, but you will get a response in sales.

In fact, you may just secure sales by plain, old-fashioned cold calling of accounts. Distributors appreciate it when you close an account and they can take over servicing the account. I have closed thousands of accounts with cold calls. It works!

Mind you, a very connected sales director achieves a high callback rate. If a manufacturer does not have industry connections, a sales director will be imperative to success.

Be in the Stores

Track your distributor's accounts. Find out who is buying your product. You or the rep should visit stores to discover to which customers your product is currently being sold. Find out if these customers are in your buyers' retail landscapes. Perhaps, after some strategic talk, you can alter your position. You might live in California, for example, but discover that your product is a hit in Connecticut or Michigan. Although it may not be feasible to personally visit those out-of-state store customers, retailers can phone them and send them coupons to show gratitude for their business. This will create buzz. You will be surprised how a little concentrated effort can impact your sales.

Watch Your Shelf Life

The shelf life for most products is roughly 365 to 450 days, after which they can no longer be sold at a retail level. Therefore, you can't ship to a distributor product close to expiration because they will know the expiration date. Of course, some people do this anyway. I witnessed one overstocked manufacturer, in a scramble to stay solvent, ship distributors $40,000 of soon-to-expire product that had been sitting in a warehouse. Sly? No. Unprofessional. The distributor doesn't want it. Another time I worked with a manufacturer that sent product to Nature's Best that was expiring within six months. Nature's Best was not impressed and three months later sent most of it back.

Do not ship product unless it is six months before your organic and normal expiration date. Product that's about to expire should be used for demos, samples, and freebies.

Also avoid overstock! Doing so will reduce the pressure to ship product too close to its expiration date. For most of its history, Amazon has labored tirelessly to reduce spiraling losses due to overwhelming inventory and overstock issues. It has systematically implemented numerous radical technologies to adjust to customer demand. You can be just as careful. I suggest you forecast your sales and produce accordingly. Stick to your plan. I understand that longer production runs will reduce costs. But don't let third parties convince you of the value of producing three or four times what your plan calls for, just to support their optimistic sales predictions for an advertised special. Running out of stock for two weeks is a lesser evil than returning $20,000 in product. It happens more than you think, so be wiser.

There is a fine line between overstock and understock. Many manufacturers overstock and think that close to the expiry date their product is still sellable. Well, it's not. So don't let yourself get stuck with unsellable expired product!

SHELF CHECK ❖ 8

Don't Do Trade Shows Without a Major Distributor

Far too often I have seen manufacturers with inflated egos but without distribution channels set up booths at conventions and leave with zero sales, empty promises, and enormous bills. In the eyes of major retailers, without a distributor you are an amateur, a wannabe—or, worse, as Mark Cuban, the owner of the Dallas Mavericks, would say, "a want-a-preneur." The majors will assume that these manufacturers will be gone in a year or two. Usually they are right.

I've seen the difference having a distributor makes. I attended a show with a manufacturer who had attended the previous year to no effect. This manufacturer came back strong with distributors locked in. The product was available and easy to order. We closed more than $20,000 in deals on the show floor.

I worked with another team who felt that because their product was so outstanding everyone at Expo would buy direct. Thinking solely about distributor costs (losing an immediate 35 percent of margin), they could not immediately look a few steps down the road. As a result, they had no sales. When I stepped in to consult, I set up distributors and retailers, and during the following year Expo generated more than $30,000 in sales on the floor.

Distributors' trade shows are your opportunity to get in the game. A spirit of deal making permeates them. You will meet distributor sales reps and buyers face-to-face. It's imperative at your incubation stage to expand your contacts. So shows are a very efficient way to secure deals. Be passionate!

Development takes as long as it needs to. Skipping any of

its steps can be fatal to a brand in infancy. The Natural Foods Expo West is the most affluent food Expo in the world and also one of the most expensive to take part in. If you go to The Natural Foods Expo West in Anaheim without a distributor and/or your product isn't shelf ready, you are bleeding unnecessary cash. Stick with the fundamentals: Partner with a distributor.

If buyers are enthusiastic about your product, they may take an order from you, but this is rare. Some retailers make decisions on the spot on the trade show floor, which resembles the noisy activity on the New York Stock Exchange floor. But usually these retailers are smaller and will do the bulk of their ordering through a distributor. Few are interested in direct sales or ordering via private sales sites.

A ll distributed products must be guaranteed as well as insured. Retailers require this insurance from distributors for a myriad of reasons: product expiration, damage, nonperformance, even product explosions. Insurance allows a distributor to secure a credit for returned product. Everyone wins. Retailers understand that manufacturers cannot always refund product, so they let distributors share risk.

Before a Review, *Secure Distribution*

Retailers rely on a process called category reviews to accomplish many things. One of their objectives, critical to you, is what is known as a "reset." A reset wholly remerchandises a category in their stores according to a planogram or design schematic. This reset is the motion picture equivalent to being nominated for an Oscar and then getting a chance to vote for yourself. I have been fortunate enough to receive an invitation to participate in a large grocery store's reset. Imagine: There is madness in the store and you are able to collaborate with the managers on exactly where your product sits. Instead of your product being on the bottom shelf, you have an opportunity to move it up to eye level. Cultivate your relationships to increase the possibility of getting an invitation to a review.

DSD (Direct Sales Distributor)

A DSD is a distributor, but it's a full-service distributor. A DSD will restock your shelves and fight tooth and nail to sell product, whereas major broadline distributors do not restock shelves, check tags, or fill voids. They simply pack pallets and deliver.

Here is how a DSD works. Let's say you are a beverage supplier and you want to get into 7-Eleven and convenience stores. To do so you decide to use a DSD. The DSD takes care of your product by ensuring tags are up, there are no voids, merchandise is correctly positioned, coupons are available, and stock levels are adequate. They become an extension of your company. They will go in and make sure your product is there. If your product is in demand, a DSD can be another set of eyes and feet on the street. But you do pay for this service with their high markups. One example of a DSD is HBC (Haralambos Beverage Company; www.haralambos.com) in Southern California. There are many other food and supplement DSDs, such as Frozen Gourmet in Northern California (www.frozengourmetinc.com), Natural Choice in Northern California (www.naturalchoicefoods.com), Lipari Foods in Michigan (www.liparifoods.com), Island Fresh in New York (www.islandfreshny.com), Cold Front Distribution in Denver (www.coldfrontdist.com), Select Nutrition in California (www.selectnutrition.com), and Dora's Natural in New York (www.dorasnaturals.com), which has become the preferred DSD distributor for New York City. This is to name just a few. I also want to mention an outstanding regional distributor, Los Angeles Distributors (better known as LAD) in Southern California (www.ladistco.com). They are a Los Angeles region distributor and not a full-service DSD. However, they give a lot of service to their customers without charging like a DSD. They have very competitive pricing. They are a great team to work with that makes every effort to take care of your product. I know this firsthand because I have and continue to work with LAD.

NOTE: Retail category review paperwork requires distributor item numbers. If you do not have a distributor, this process of acceptance will be most difficult. Though not impossible to sell directly to retailers, your chances increase with preferred distributors.

Advantages of DSDs

DSDs make sense—to some. From the perspective of a traditional small store, this can be true. A DSD like HBC has an in-house sales group that goes out to sell your product at their thousands of retail accounts. You can ride along with their sales team. If you are a success with a DSD you are on the way to brand recognition. Your product will be easily recognized because it's in convenience stores, liquor stores, independent grocers, cafeterias, gift stores, car washes, gas stations, and many more locations. Prompted by sales data demonstrating your DSD's success, retailers will more likely request a major distributor to supply your product.

Another advantage of DSDs is that there is no minimum order for retailers. Most major distributors have a minimum order of $500. For many little liquor stores that's just too large for a weekly or biweekly order. But DSDs will not only sell any size order but also merchandise, stock, and restock products. A DSD is full service, which means if your product is delivered, the DSD salespeople ensure it gets on the shelf.

Disadvantages of DSDs

In recent years, it has become very costly for suppliers to get into a DSD. DSD upcharge can be up to about 40%. Honestly, suppliers end up giving too much away. This can be an alluring and additional source of revenue, but have your team examine this path very carefully. A DSD may sound attractive because it has 4,000 accounts, but the hassle is the small size of these accounts. A DSD rep will drive endlessly around presenting to one small account after another only to face tightfisted buyers and conservative family-run stores. These types of retailers are rarely open to new products because they have a tiny store and don't want the risk of a new, untried product.

DSD accounts more often than not don't have the money of a WFM or a Sprouts and therefore can't always pay full price. For example, they may be interested in coconut water because it's a proven product people request but not interested in the new Stevia-sweetened tea unless it's at the right price or is even a steal. Most specialty products are too expensive for DSDs. If a DSD retailer's normal price for a drink is about $1, then a $3 specialty drink will sit there gathering dust. Plus all DSD retailers want free-fills and often take the free product and don't reorder. Also, DSDs require opening deals like buying one and getting one free. So when that deal ends perhaps your sales end as well. This is often how little products fall between the cracks of DSDs.

Compare that to getting national distribution for a thousand Safeway accounts across the United States set up with UNFI distributors who have distribution centers nationwide. This can be done using a systematic review schedule with one presentation for all 1,000 accounts. It's like a hole in one. So you can see why DSDs are a bottom-feeder type of game unless you have the "breakout," in-demand, super-new product at every corner store in the country.

An example of a breakout DSD item is 5-hour ENERGY. This product was the first in its category on the market. It was a breakout hit that had every corner store in the country foaming at the mouth for supplies. This is one case where a DSD was great because the small accounts had access to 5-hour ENERGY along with their minimum order. DSDs fill in the cracks that big distributors miss. But I can assure you that for every one hit product there are a thousand misses.

Major retailers tend not to use DSDs as much as major distributors because DSDs tend to cover territories rather than national chains or not to have as wide a range of products and categories as the majors. Buyers from big retailers buy from DSDs a little here and there, but when they want to place their major orders they buy from the big guns with the big selections.

> Your website is important for direct sales. But a website is an absolute necessity for any product business to succeed. Your product and website must be launched simultaneously.

Going It Alone

There is a different way to start a customer base: direct sales. If you get a direct sale with a major retailer you keep the 35 percent profit that would otherwise go to the distributor. Those savings in turn can be reinvested in ads, sales, and/or demos, which will please the retailers. However, think carefully about direct sales as a tactic. If a beverage company relies on direct sales, the heavy weight will make the beverages expensive to ship in small quantities to retailers. Such shipping costs increase operating expenses. On the other hand, distributors purchase in volume and they do the shipping but will charge you for their services. Pallet purchases (i.e., larger volumes) through direct sales are rare, but if possible charge ahead!

It's true that major retailers own distribution centers and do order directly to warehouse from product suppliers rather than distributors. But as a rule, this is reserved for high-volume products. For instance, a major beverage company I worked for distributes its product to WFM via UNFI. Given its size, this beverage company has every right to approach WFM directly and offer pallet discounts because large savings are inevitable for all involved.

You may not have a high-performing item. Or you may have a product just launched. In general, I would say that an effective distributor route is the best method for most retailers.

E-Commerce Website

Direct sales can start right from your website. When considering the development of your site, hire experts and the best your budget can afford. Many companies keep track of their online sales and analyze sales data closely. Setting up a website is a necessary step while preparing for distribution. Various forms of data stemming from online sales analysis will add immense value to your endeavor. Today, more than ever, success stories you share with your potential distributors via Twitter, Facebook, and other outlets will demonstrate your professionalism.

Have a store locator on your website. This will allow your ultimate customers to know where they can find your product. Offer online coupons and loyalty programs. And, above all, listen to your customers and invite them to join the process of growing your business. Once you garner true customers, they will be a voice supporting you in the marketplace.

Be realistic about what you expect of your website. It's rare, at least in the natural products industry, that a product can be a success solely through online sales. You need to remember that most stores and chains want a distributor to supply products so as to ensure quality service and guarantees. This is precisely why distributors are a necessary partnership!

> For consumers, the changing retail landscape is both welcome and annoying. After all, it's human nature to resist change, especially when not on our own terms.

SHELF SPACE

How to Own
Your Retail Shelf Space

Every square foot of a retail location must generate income. Algorithms and assistant managers continually reshape these retail environments, looking for profit. Turnover is the rule, so suppliers with the highest sales, most ads, and brand awareness evolve into superstars—if they can keep up product support and sales numbers. If a product doesn't perform, stores get rid of it. If you want to get your product onto retail shelves, you need to understand why a product stays on shelves and what gets it thrown off.

Authorization Does Not Equal Sales

Authorization into a store is a wonderful moment. You've fulfilled your mission and you can brag, "Hey! We are in ____ stores!" Also, being authorized to place product in multiple stores will let you leverage discussions with other retailers, buyers, and brokers.

But an authorization does not guarantee sales. That's because an authorization does not mean your product will end up on the shelf, consistently, and in a favorable spot. And getting on a shelf in a good position is still only half the battle. A standout undeniable product generating good sales volume is the other half—that will protect you from trips to the discount bin.

What Is a Good Placement?

Given the pressure to produce sales, your product must be well placed on store shelves. What's well placed? Your goal is to have your product at eye level. To obtain this, stay committed but don't be a difficult visitor to a store. Before store visits, prioritize your goals and think through your plan. Immediately asking for an eye-level placement can be seen as unrealistic, so be cautious at the outset of the relationship. Like water, you can flow around rock.

Of great importance when you do secure authorizations is

immediately supervising the initial cut-in onto shelves. When I refer to cut-in I mean *on the shelf with a tag*. And many employees will let you help them.

Each store has unique protocols for activities such as shipping to them and receiving by them. Your team will need to have a basic checklist to remember these protocols.

Equally important is following up after shipment of your product. Remember, there are thousands of products—you are not the only vendor. Once (store) authorizations have been secured and initial orders have been filled, your follow-up plan of action must ensure that your product will have shelf life. And there are not many limitations to what other vendors might do when a brand ambassador is not present. I'll discuss these in more depth later.

With the endless flow of new products into a typical store receiving area, new-to-the-store product often may sit idle on a shelf or hidden behind another box. So your brand ambassador or sales rep must, at times, literally retrieve the product from receiving and get it onto shelves. Then a shelf tag must be obtained from an employee. Usually there are one or two people who are responsible for shelf tags, and you have to find them to get a tag. Getting the tags alone will keep a portion of your competitors at bay.

Here's a trick to impress retailers with your product. When your product is finally cut in, most employees are aware of its arrival. Keep them aware of your product. On your first follow-up, arrive with product samples and educate the store, staff, and *owners*. Be sure to budget for this expense. It is vital that employees walking by your product hours on end be willing to endorse it. On occasion, employees can end up being your most loyal customers. I've blitzed many retailers by giving away product and educating staff and customers about the product, retaining sales long after the visit.

A Constant Watch

After the initial cut-in, you may find your product missing again after two or three weeks. Be cautious and do not allow your emotions to get out of hand. Remember, you need to cultivate your in-store relationships.

As Woody Allen once said, "80 percent of success is showing up." Being a physical presence in stores is essential. Without a constant neighborhood watch you will lose your spot as fast as you got it.

For example, I was working for a manufacturer that had closed over 100 accounts, and rather quickly, I might add. There was a palpable enthusiasm for the product among all players. All new accounts required free-fills, often a necessary evil. However, the assumption the manufacturer made was that the free-fill would secure the manufacturer's spot. But months later, I made a store visit only to find product not on shelves.

There are at least ten reasons why product disappears from the shelves:

1. Product is in the back.
You become Indiana Jones. You unearth your product, buried under a sea of other products. Typically, store staff will help you refill your shelf space.

2. A competing brand ambassador removed your tag.
Equivalent to street bullying. It does not happen frequently, but enough. Certain promotion cycles bring out this type of behavior in competitors. So grit your teeth, reset your tags—and do not reciprocate. Rise above and be sure to sink both foul shots!

3. The tag fell off.
It happens.

4. You sold out!
You literally sold out. Which would be great news, except none of the employees recall your product, no tag was created, and another product has moved into your spot.

5. The product was never received.
This happens more than it should. Orders get lost, but that's just part of the game, so stay on top of your orders.

6. The store did not have time to cut in your product.

Annoying, but common. Make it happen.

7. The reset was delayed, and your delivery date was pushed back.

This is common with resets. Resets are scheduled for one date and happen four weeks later. Be patient, but firm.

8. Someone rearranged the shelves, and your product was left out.

Shelves are rearranged and items are squeezed out. The higher your sales, the less likely this will happen to you.

9. The retailer cuts your product!

This happens as a result of underperformance, period, and often occurs with no warning or notice.

10. The distributor is out of product.

Sometimes your product runs out and you are unaware of it until it's too late. It happens to the best of us. We can't bear the burden of everything, so find the humor in the situation and keep your chin up. There are worse problems to have than your product being too high in demand. One thing you can do is keep close tabs on your distributors to keep this situation from happening again.

L ook closely at the shelves and fridges of WFM, Sprouts, and other major "natural grocers" and you will see majors releasing natural lines. These major companies may acquire successful natural companies or develop their own. Either way the competition is fierce. So be fierce! If you are, they will be acquiring you in three to five years. Yes—bought out!

Renters of the Retail World

Being a "renter" is where you start in stores. It's like having an apartment, and you do have a lease. But the lease is month to month, so the landlord (i.e., the chain) could decide that they no longer want your product. So being a "renter" is not where you want to finish! Starting as a renter of shelf space is your way in. Eventually you want to establish a place on the shelves of your accounts that you feel you "own."

The good news is, there's always room for a renter in any store. But rental locations will be poor and most likely overlooked. Given the poor placements, it's no surprise there will be a high turnover in the renter's world. But because of this turnover, for the retailer, renters have a place in their business model. Renters and their product lines offer competition against leading brands that own their established space. Renters and owners both have to pay for expensive ads, demos, and slotting fees. So you can see why turnovers are somewhat desirable to retailers. If a product dies on the vine it's replaced by the next rental product. There will be no lack of entrepreneurs in the world who are vying for your spot and more than willing to pay cash for it. Retailers make money from this type of restaurant-style turnover. Before we talk about how you end up being an "owner," let's have a look at the issues you can face as you struggle to get an established space on store shelves.

I met with a hundred-store gas station I'll call X-Pensive. X-Pensive was a high-volume and coveted account with Core-Mark. After a fantastic meeting, X-Pensive offered a rollout of forty stores. The price was a free-fill for four SKUs and a $400/store slotting fee. In all, a price tag of $19,000. I politely declined. There is no way any company can profit from such a high price. If you are made an offer like this, I don't care how much you want the account, don't do it!

As a Renter, Beware of High-Performance-or-You-Are-"Out" Traps

A high-performance-or-you-are-"out" trap is designed so that few succeed and many fail. This is a very expensive trap indeed, costing upward of $20,000. Some retailers have a portion of their business model designed to profit immensely off naive renters. Nonrefundable slotting fees are usually a one-time charge to get shelf space. For major established brands it's well worth the investment. However, for renters it's a battle to make the numbers to keep their shelf space. So a high turnover of renters with unestablished brands can be quite profitable for some retailers.

If you view the world through rose-colored glasses, you will find retailers that appear to be no less than the Holy Grail. They are easy to spot. They have extraordinary locations in their stores for renters, usually in very high-traffic and touristy centers. For a few suppliers, they are the lifeblood of their cash flow, and the store is a constant high-performing account. But for the other 90 percent of vendors, they are high-rent money pits. Many of these retailers will tell you that if you pay the slotting fees, ads, discounts, and free-fill you're in the club. But once your rental space is secured, store executives will place impossible sales minimums on you within your first six months.

You must be well established to perform in these spaces, and if you can achieve the sales levels you will thrive. But if you don't, these retailers profit enormously from your demise.

Smaller beverage companies notoriously fall into this trap. While I was working for a beverage company, one retailer said to us, "We'll give you six months if you free-fill our stores and provide deep discounts with an aggressive demo campaign. If you perform in the top ten of our beverages, then we keep you—simple." Now, we should have known better because when we walked into these accounts there were already several items in the 50-percent-off bin. They were that week's fallen soldiers and it was their rental space we had just taken over.

Yet despite such warnings, we forged ahead. The shelves were stocked with our beverage, demos raged on in full force, and discounts flew around like monkeys in *The Wizard of Oz*. The product sold at demos, but when the circus was over, customers stopped buying. At six months they cut us, so thousands of dollars of vital operating cash were burned up chasing a phantom. The slow and steady climber will achieve greater results faster and will have more operating cash available.

Owners

So how do you get to be an "owner," a product that is so established that it is very difficult for the competition to take your shelf space away from you? You must pay your dues by being a success and proving your financial strength. But that is no guarantee of continuing "ownership" of your shelf space. To really be an owner your product needs a proven track record. This means your product is selling 365 days of the year rain or shine because it's an established, recognizable brand people come in to buy. It means your product will be selling on deal and off deal because people find it undeniable and they don't want to be without it.

Examples of brands whose shelf space is close to impregnable are such household names as Campbell's soup, Ruffles chips, Pringles chips, Coca-Cola, and Kraft Macaroni & Cheese. Their long-standing reputation, backed up by big marketing budgets, makes them difficult targets to knock off the shelf. It can be done, but probably not by you while you are getting established.

Impressing and winning over the staff on a store level is like having allies on the battlefield. Train your team to be sleuths. You want them always procuring information about trends, customer habits, and upcoming promotions. Customers often ask store staff for their opinions about products. If retail employees love your product, they will sell it. It never hurts to give them a T-shirt or two, because what better advertisement than that?

Having Enough SKUs

Earlier we covered how vital it is to launch with at least three to five SKUs so as not to be ultimately lost on the shelves. Just having two SKUs is asking for trouble. I remember one launch with this problem. One of the two SKUs was defined by the retailer as a supplement and the other as a grocery item. Customers were unable to grasp and see both products as one brand. One SKU was placed in the cash-out area, while in the supplements area the second was never really noticed. The final act of self-destruction was that all in-store advertisements focused solely on the cash-out product.

Splitting your brand between two categories on an initial launch is like inviting the Grim Reaper to your event.

Learning in the Small Chains

Launching a new product is a very exciting moment and it should be. It's often a dream come true. But over and over I have seen reality quickly set in. Orders go up and all of a sudden you have 150+ stores as customers, and then just as quickly orders drop and you lose customers. Or worse, without warning retailers pull your product midlaunch and toss you into a discount bin. A new line will replace you fast.

So team up with retailers that make the most sense for your product so you have the best shot at developing staying power and a win. Smaller retail chains of twenty stores or fewer can create success for your brand during your initial phase.

Let me give you an example. The Southern California market is one of the most coveted. There are also several small chains outside of Southern California making waves and proving great partners. Proving your brand with sales figures will be paramount. You must build a track record if you want acceptance into luxury accounts such as Sprouts Farmers Market. And, of course, the highly successful juggernaut WFM. So start with the independent chains. These are some of the most successful:

- ❖ Mother's Market & Kitchen
- ❖ Clark's Nutrition & Natural Foods Market
- ❖ Lassens Natural Foods & Vitamins
- ❖ Jimbo's . . . *Naturally!*
- ❖ Keil's
- ❖ Gelson's Markets
- ❖ Bristol Farms
- ❖ Erewhon
- ❖ Barons Market
- ❖ New Leaf Community Markets
- ❖ Andronico's Community Markets
- ❖ Better Health Store

- ❖ AKiN'S and Chamberlain's Natural Foods

- ❖ Jetro Cash & Carry (wholesale!)

- ❖ Down to Earth Organic & Natural

- ❖ Good Earth Natural Foods

- ❖ Woodman's Markets

- ❖ Huckleberry's Natural Market

- ❖ Sendik's Food Market

- ❖ Festival Foods

- ❖ Sunrise Health Foods

- ❖ Metropolitan Market

- ❖ New Frontiers Natural Marketplace

A s I said, chains of twenty stores or fewer are a good place to start. Think of these as training grounds. Inside the store is where you can learn about customer acquisition, customer interaction with products, and how to get would-be consumers to spend their money on your product. Train your team to be sleuths. You want it always procuring information about trends, customer habits, and upcoming promotions.

It is in these smaller settings that you can learn to build productive relationships and meet the challenges that must be addressed. Specifically, you need to remember that you are not the only vendor. Although a noncompeting category product is not your immediate foe, its representative, brand ambassador, regional manager, or owners still compete for face time with department heads. Be considerate of store and departmental managers, who are always overwhelmed with their own daily tasks, goals, and merchandising concerns. In the midst of all that "noise," how do you get noticed? Keep your store visits friendly and straight to the point, and walk with your store partners around the store. They have to be moving, so you must move.

SHELF CHECK ❖ 11

Don't Expect to Land Major Accounts in the First 90 Days!

Your brand will need real success stories, customer buzz, and sales data to prove you are a force to be reckoned with. So walk before you run. Don't burn up your cash chasing the giants at the start. I discuss negative cash flow later and how it paralyzes the momentum you and your team have built. But for now, we must be clear about this point: Stay away from the majors, at least for now.

Don't Go to the 1,000+ Chains with Your Product in Just Mom-and-Pop Stores

Don't approach larger chains such as Kroger, Circle K, Meijer, Lipari Foods, and Publix even once you have secured more than 100+ small-box or independent accounts. It will be a total waste of time. Many owners, founders, and directors believe they are entitled to be in a 1,000+ account chain after a small success and little to no sales data from major retail accounts. There is a time and place for accounts such as Publix. That's after you have closed at least 500+ accounts with two to three major 100+ chains with supporting SPINS data.

Retailers want unfiltered raw numbers, meaning nothing altered because you want to look good in front of a buyer. Major retailers do not want to hear inaccurate data, inflated sales data, and vague hearsay stories from the street from CEOs, brokers, and sales directors. If your product passed through registers at a natural or specialty retailer store, this information is reported to SPINS (www.spins.com). Only very small natural store chains (one to two stores) don't report to SPINS. Major retailers have a symbiotic relationship with SPINS and will quickly realize if your data are not real.

I suggest a membership to SPINS as you implement your sales strategy. You can run reports on any category and compare your sales data to your competitors'. Knowledge is power. Find out how you stand up against your competition and gain leverage for closing deals.

Once your data are in line with the expectations of high-profile targets, your industry partners, such as KeHE and UNFI, can help you in meetings with them.

It would be no surprise that some manufacturers completely fabricate sales numbers in order to close accounts and obtain financial partners and investors. However, *anyone* can obtain a SPINS data membership. So entrepreneurs, make sure your sales claims are supported by undebatable raw data.

SHELF CHECK ❖ 13

Find Your Way Slowly but Surely

I move slowly and methodically when it comes to rolling out a product. I picture a product's current position and forecast six months into the venture and work to make that reality appear. If you build up carefully, you can get yourself to the point where you can safely think about getting bigger.

So what is the point you need to reach to have a chance

with the major-league accounts? You need to have distribution with KeHE, UNFI, and Nature's Best; an effective online site; and 500+ stores as customers. WFM, Sprouts, Raley's, H-E-B, Albertsons, SUPERVALUE, Kroger, Ralphs, Vitamin Cottage, Safeway, Super Supplements, Publix, Publix GreenWise Markets, and Vons are among the most-coveted accounts.

W FM has a list of unapproved ingredients regarding its products. This list is updated regularly. Become familiar with it because it will help you survive WFM reviews.

Category Reviews

Major retailers such as Publix, Walgreens, and Kroger are very large, some with 1,000+ stores. You should know that if you do get them as accounts you will be subject to their mandatory category reviews. Categories include supplements, grocery, nonfoods, hygiene, dairy, fresh baked, super fruits, produce, apparel—on and on the list goes. Acceptance can often be the decision of a jury, not just a buyer.

A category review will examine all of the products in a category to identify the sellers, and the ones that need to be replaced by a new product. Reviews may be conducted by a panel rather than just a category buyer. Category reviews are spread out over a calendar year so reviews are not all on the same day. In fact, they are weeks apart throughout the year. Review schedules are coveted because they are not public knowledge and are not readily available online. You must be invited or you won't be considered. You can obtain a copy of the review calendar through retailers, buyers, brokers, and/or your sales director. These groups of people overlap and are in constant contact—all sharing information in real time. If you are not in the "in group," hire someone who is.

The Journey onto the WFM Shelves

Getting onto the shelves of the huge natural foods chain WFM is not as simple as taking an order over the phone and submitting it to UNFI.

WFM buyers do not want to force new products into each store, but with authorization you can sell to the stores. If a grocery manager or a Whole Body section and supplement manager accepts your product, then that individual store will generate a simple PO. However, getting that PO from one specific store is in the middle of a chain of events that generally looks like the following:

❖ Once you get authorization for your product, it will be listed in the WFM data site called IRMA.

- ❖ To get a meeting at store level, you should say to the grocery manager or the Whole Body manager, "We are authorized in your region. You can check in IRMA and buy through UNFI West."

- ❖ Face-to-face meetings should be booked at each store in the approved regions.

- ❖ A PO should be obtained from each store. WFM generates an internal PO number, which is the number you give UNFI with your WFM turnover. When your product is delivered, the PO on the invoice is matched up at the WFM delivery area. If the PO case count doesn't match and/or the PO number doesn't exist, the delivery will be rejected at your expense.

- ❖ Product is shipped through UNFI.

UNFI codes are divided into two categories: East USA and West USA. The UNFI West code is the code that all UNFI West customers can use to order. The UNFI East code is the code that all UNFI East customers can use to order. East codes can't be used for West and West codes can't be used for East.

So let's look at the first step in the chain: getting an authorization. To be authorized by WFM regional buyer(s), unless an established relationship exists, you will most likely need to make a face-to-face presentation. Each region approves or disapproves items. This is precisely why a well-connected sales director or broker can present product and acquire authorization.

Once you obtain a PO, fill out a form called a turnover. UNFI and Nature's Best require turnovers to be submitted online to their ordering department. Do not send orders until product stock is in the distributor's warehouse *and* ready to ship. UNFI requires POs only with its WFM orders. For your other UNFI accounts, you need to supply only account numbers. One reason for this is that to date WFM has required an additional PO to go with its turnovers. Another reason is that if WFM didn't require a PO, then let's face it, a frenzy of products would be sent to WFM without permission. Without a PO number it would be next to impossible for WFM to keep track of its deliveries.

NOTE: If you miss a delivery appointment at UNFI and/or Nature's Best, you are not allowed to just show up later. Deliveries are tightly scheduled at the docking area, which is open Monday through Friday from

3 a.m. to 11 a.m. Appointments are often scheduled at least a week out. UNFI and Nature's Best have an extremely busy schedule, so lateness is not tolerated, nor should it be.

So that is the basic process that you go through with one store.

Of course, with authorization you can approach all of WFM's individual stores in a region with codes, pricing, and the SRP (suggested retail price). Your product has been accepted by UNFI and is ready for coding. Once a WFM regional buyer confirms authorization, UNFI issues codes with SRP and unit price, information buyers need to know. (I should mention that UNFI will not order until it gets at least eight to ten customer POs.)

Next, product ships through UNFI. Wait—not so fast! It is important to know that UNFI requires a major retailer commitment before it will accept your product into each distribution center. For example, you will need a commitment from all fifty-four of WFM's South Pacific stores before the Moreno Valley UNFI distribution center will accept you as a supplier. With WFM, this is the chicken-and-egg scenario at its finest—meaning do you get into UNFI first or WFM first? The answer is yes. UNFI codes your item, and this code will be the item number WFM will use to access item numbers in its system.

This is also the number all UNFI Moreno Valley account customers can use to order your item.

Unfortunately, you will still have a problem. You will have no product at the UNFI Moreno Valley warehouse for one to two months. I suggest letting the stores know their PO may take one to two months to fill. This is not an unusual situation for a new product, and WFM knows it. WFM team leaders will understand their PO's expected date of delivery. Although this can be a common issue, good communication is key to overcoming this hurdle.

NOTE: All WFMs require a free-fill, which is usually a case of product. They don't require slotting fees but they do require at least two rounds of demos. For coveted accounts it's a steal and well worth it! This is a prize account, so treat it like the royalty it is. If you lack sales at WFMs after six months of placement, then you have a problem. Refer to the discussion about black holes in Chapter 8.

Now, how do you get beyond your first region? You will need to get approvals from the appropriate buyer for other regions because you can only sell into approved WFM regions. For example, if you are approved only for South Pacific but you happen to be in Colorado, you will not be authorized for that region unless the Rocky Mountain WFM buyer authorizes you.

Other WFM regions can access your sales numbers, which gives you leverage when trying to get accepted by other WFM regions and additional UNFI distribution centers. Timeline for this? It will typically take a year or two to expand to different regions. Once you are in three or four WFM regions and are performing, you may consider global review or simply continue to expand into other regions.

As you move forward with WFM, you can bring your success stories to other retailers like Sprouts, Raley's, and other 100+ chains. With a great product and positive SPINS data, they will let you in the game.

WFM Category Reviews

WFM category reviews occur at both the global and regional level. When presenting to WFM you need to set realistic goals. I worked with three companies that all made the same mistake. I'll use Michael's Perfect Pickles as an example. Michael thought his Perfect Pickles were so fantastic that all twelve WFM regions would agree to bring in his product. Michael instructed his team to present to WFM's global review. Yet there was no data to back up his expectation and, in fact, Michael's Perfect Pickles had not sold in one WFM store. He went to the review and submitted his pickles. As time passed Michael expectantly waited for the call, which never came. Nobody calls you to reject—only to accept.

The three companies all experienced the same failure. However, for one I was quietly setting up WFM regional review paperwork for the South Pacific region simply because this is where I am located and could give it my complete attention. (Major retailers respond to local vendors because they get personal attention while supporting the community and local employers.) I also advised caution, telling the company that if we went for broke and attacked the Death Star, we might not have a single win. The client requested that I not submit for the South Pacific region because he thought it a waste of our time to close one WFM region and told me that my work conflicted with his global review strategy. At a trade show six months later, I met with a WFM regional buyer who recalled that application. With a chuckle, he said he had rarely experienced twelve WFM regional buyers agreeing on *any product*, especially unproven ones. "Why would you waste your time?" was his question. He advised me to go after just one region at a time.

Even if Michael's Perfect Pickles was accepted into the South Pacific region, it wouldn't mean he was an "auto ship" to the thirty-three retail locations. He would discover that he would need to sell into each individual WFM store in the South Pacific region one by one—*argh*! Now that's a big stipulation, and acceptance by the region is no guarantee that all or any of the WFM South Pacific retail locations would accept product or keep it.

NOTE: All products that you want to sell in WFM must be authorized and activated by WFM headquarters. Each regional buyer will input product into the WFM database IRMA. Once you are accepted, you are allowed to sell it in any of the region's stores. However, it's often up to you to get it on the shelves at a store level.

Never Submit a WFM Turnover Before Stock Is in a UNFI Distribution Center

Anytime you are submitting orders for UNFI for any region, first call customer service to ensure that product is there. Your item code and distribution center name are all you need to obtain this information.

Murphy's Law operates in the food industry, just as it does anywhere else. A few years back, I had a confirmed delivery appointment at UNFI. My truck was late, the logistics company did not report that it had missed my appointment, and subsequently I was denied delivery.

Imagine my disappointment when I submitted turnovers to UNFI thinking my product was in the warehouse only to find that WFM had not received product! I called into UNFI and they told me they were out of stock and didn't know if and when product was expected to arrive. To make matters worse, since WFM POs expire once they are submitted, the POs were closed. I had to return to all the stores and beg for a new PO. Avoid this frustration.

However, don't assume all is well even after delivery. At times, it can take three days to log in new products due to the high volume of data. This is especially true with WFM. When a store receives a shipment, it matches it with the delivered UNFI PO and WFM's PO. If the two POs don't match the shipment, it will be rejected by the store.

If you are around 500+ accounts, you are a potentially valuable account for a broker. So even before this benchmark, a broker courtship should commence. Brokers should be your path to buyers and distributors to expand your business. And so it begins, a courtship of brokers—a place where many succeed and many more are burned!

6

BROKERS

What You
Need to Know

L et's say you're doing well six months after your brand has launched. You have at least 500 accounts, and sales are not stagnant. You own your space in stores; that is, you aren't in immediate danger of being sent to the bargain bin. You are in a continual dialogue with all your industry partners. Going forward, you will be emphasizing ongoing sales and brand awareness, and you see 2,000 accounts in the next half year as an achievable goal. Independents such as you create grassroots success all the time. One major chain authorization will trigger additional authorizations. It is at this point that you should begin to consider the use of a broker.

A broker can be your sherpa, but you also have to be wary.

Although a broker can lead you up the mountain and protect you, brokers know that not everyone summits. Manufacturers come and go, and trends dominate the marketplace. As one manufacturer exits, another arrives fresh off the assembly line. Long-term relationships between brokers and manufacturers can be rare. So be realistic about your expectations of a broker and protect yourself at all times.

> I once overheard a broker at a major KeHE trade show say, "Look at all these fantastic booths and exciting new products. Next year, half of them won't be here." And it's true.

Don't Worry About Having a Broker for Development or Launches

Although brokers have an important role, don't rush to get one. Brokers are not required for product development or brand launch, nor do you need one before you have 500 accounts, because brokers charge excessively to *develop* a brand. Manufacturers with unproven brands will be charged monthly retainer fees upward of $6,000 by major brokers and $2,000 by boutique brokers. Additionally, brokers are not vested in your company. Brokers represent many manufacturers. You will lose your shirt waiting on brokers to capture every relationship and account. Brokers will not operate on your timeline, and, in fact, they use time to their advantage. Returning calls? Not their strong point. So using brokers too soon will siphon precious operating cash. There are a few, but not many, brokers who will ethically represent a product with no secured accounts and/or brand awareness upon signing. Some brokers might jump in early if an established brand launches a secondary product line. Otherwise, it's not worth their time working on a brand they have to pioneer; that's your job! They perform best by maintaining an established product while expanding its reach.

What is the alternative? For day-to-day operations, hire a sales director. Experienced sales directors know how to manage, communicate, and create productivity with overlapping teams. However, note that this is a serious decision because of its longer-term implications. When you are ready to expand, at some point, you will be faced with the question of whether your sales director has the skills needed to manage a much larger sales team, including regional vice presidents. You will need a real impact leader to take this role. You may need to let go of less capable people.

Watch Out for Desperate Boutique Brokers!

Many boutique brokers tend to be a bit desperate, and some will say anything to get your business. They do this because they only get the smaller fish, and they need a lot of them to feed on because most of the smaller manufacturers have very short shelf lives. The big fish will go with the major brokers who have lots of clients, don't need to lie to get your business, and turn down half of the manufacturers who apply to partner with them.

So let's imagine the pitch a somewhat desperate boutique broker might give to a manufacturer of a new unproven product: "Hey, I've seen your product everywhere in the independents. Glad we are on board to support your first major authorization—wow, Whole Foods!" This all sounds positive, but after the cheerful banter, empty promises, and 400 days at exorbitant rates, few tangible results will have appeared.

SHELF CHECK ❖ 16

Ask Potential Brokers if They Can Solve Your Biggest Problem(s)

One of the best ways to judge a relationship is how your problems are dealt with. For example, Michael's Perfect Pickles has more than 500 accounts, including a couple of majors such as WFM and Sprouts. When Michael reviews his SPINS reports, he discovers that several Sprouts locations are not selling Michael's Bread and Butter flavor although the SKU is authorized. This is what we call "gaps in distribution."

Personal account visits could rectify this problem. But with Michael's heavy schedule of trade shows and buyer meetings, he's not sure how to solve the problem efficiently. Most broker account executives are in and out of major accounts every week on all sorts of business. Account executives may have a list of fifty products to discuss at each retailer, but as long as they achieve your goals that will be what matters. Michael tells a broker he is interviewing, "My biggest problem is that fifty-some Sprouts stores are missing our Bread and Butter SKU. We need to solve this fast. Can you fix Sprouts' gap in distribution within a month?" If the broker assures Michael that he or she can meet his goal, Michael's response should be, "Let's put this in our agreement because this is important for success."

Take advantage of midseason replacements. For example, if your product is authorized at a major chain, you can set up additional SKUs for it if it is doing well at your independent accounts. Book a meeting with the buyer even if you are months from another category review, and suggest replacing a stagnant SKU with the new one. Offer incentives with ads, sales, and demos. A great broker can easily facilitate midseason replacements.

Gaps In Distribution

As I noted in Shelf Check 16, "gaps in distribution" means you have authorization to be placed in a store(s) and for one reason or another your product isn't there. Imagine Michael's Perfect Pickles is now authorized in all Sprouts stores. But one day while Michael is in Phoenix, Arizona, he discovers that several of the Sprouts stores don't have two of the four authorized SKUs. A good broker and sales team can resolve this quickly.

Distribution gaps can plague a product launch. So stay close to make sure you don't have any gaps.

Your retail buyer might see only overall sales numbers and decide that yours is a poorly performing product when in fact it's really the gaps that are dragging your numbers down. For example, if you are authorized for 150 stores and only 75 actually receive your product, you won't have true sales numbers. If you were in all the stores, your sales might double. So you must fix this problem fast.

What would happen to your product otherwise? Buyers might simply cut it and support someone else's. They will offer your space to new brands or, worse, expand your direct competition as midseason replacements. And if another manufacturer approaches them with an undeniable product, large ad budget, marketing plan, and deep pockets, watch out!

So how do you defend yourself? You need to dig deeper into the sales data and demonstrate that once you improve distribution your sales might double. Improve your distribution quickly, and present the positive sales data in SPINS reports. Until your brand builds a die-hard fan base, you must guard shelves meticulously. Loyal customers are the goal. Become undeniable.

Just because your product is undeniable, however, doesn't mean it's irreplaceable. I stumbled upon some chocolate-covered pomegranate ice cream bars at Ralphs once and bought them for a party. That night, several of us ate the bars and found them decadent. They were our new favorite! Three weeks later Ralphs underwent a reset and these ice cream bars were cut. This happens frequently. So one can never get too comfortable.

10 Ways to Avoid Being Broken by a Broker

1. Thoroughly research as many brokers as possible— and get references.

2. Avoid broker burn.

3. Ask potential brokers to disclose their account lists.

4. Discover how many account executives are in the broker-age and what its coverage is.

5. Ask how often the potential broker visits retail accounts.

6. Discover how accessible buyers are to you and how often the potential broker meets with them.

7. Find out what other products the potential broker represents and whether there are any conflicts.

8. Determine whether the potential broker supports clients at trade shows.

9. Find out if the potential broker charges a percentage or a retainer.

10. Outline the conditions of the agreement and termination.

1. Thoroughly Research as Many Brokers as Possible— and Get References

Start your broker search inside your current accounts network. Talk to retail managers and ask which brokers they prefer and why. Who do they see the most often? Who do they highly respect? An outstanding broker is known inside store accounts. An outstanding broker diligently works shelves, presents new items, and resolves issues with integrity. I have been told, "Broker John Doe from ABC Company is here every week and he's fantastic." Distributors are another good resource to assess brokers. They can recommend top brokers tailored to your brand. WFM corporate offices supply a list of recommended national and regional brokers.

Does your broker work with buyers in your desired category? Specificity is key. If your broker works mainly with food items, then your new toothpaste item is a misfit. If you are launching a skin-care line, just authorized at the WFM Whole Body department in the South Pacific region, then make it a priority to visit the WFM Whole Body department and ask the Whole Body team leader, "Who is your best Whole Body broker for skin-care products?" Brokers might not have a working relationship with buyers in every category. If one broker doesn't have the buyer you need, continue your search. Be smart. You don't want to finance your broker's networking efforts unless they pay off for you. Treat this process as if you were hiring a babysitter—which you are!

2. Avoid Broker Burn

Brokers are unusual creatures. There must be some underground society and a cave somewhere on this planet where they have annual meetings. Google Maps might not be able to find it, but I am convinced it exists. They are, at times, highly unreachable. Let me be candid about this kind of relationship. I call it "broker burn." There are brokers who will say all the right things to get your commitment. Dare I use a car salesman analogy here? Nah.

Once you contract this type of broker, your calls are rarely returned. Excuses, scheduling problems, and multiple dodge-and-evade tactics will be employed against you. Before signing, treat *any* agreement with brokers as though you were signing a new mobile carrier contract in the remote mountainous regions of Pakistan.

They say it's not the years, but the mileage. Trade shows

have the ability to age you by a year in just a few days. One quickly gauges personalities stalking any trade show floor. Character after character goes by, swimming past booths more than once. Some characters are genuine. Others smell like sea lice. Then there are the sharks, looking for prey such as fresh founders, obviously delusional owners, and starry-eyed salespeople.

So let's use Michael's Perfect Pickles as an example of a real-life client I once had at a trade show. Unfortunately, other brokers were not eager to sign Michael's brand at that moment. Reputable brokers had rejected the brand. Michael's problem? Sales numbers.

A brokerage president swims over to Michael's trade show booth. "Chuck" (the broker's fictional name, to protect the "innocent") raves about potential possibilities and spews out his retail buyers' names, from WFM, Sprouts, Nugget Markets, Bristol Farms, and Raley's to Albertsons. As conversation continues, Michael's team is cautious due to Chuck's hefty $2,000 or 6 percent of manufacturer's sales rate. With a non-performance contract structure, Chuck would be entitled to his monthly retainer regardless of results. Michael cringes at this fee.

However, Chuck claims his brokerage can get Michael's Perfect Pickles accepted into major accounts, if they work together. Michael imagines no harm in Chuck just presenting Michael's to potential accounts and agrees to support this goal.

Sometime later, after supposedly presenting Michael's Perfect Pickles, Chuck announces he has more than 150 accounts ready to authorize. If we will come aboard contractually, Chuck will close deals and bring in product to major buyer reviews.

Alas, a deal is executed. With Chuck's team on board, supposedly the sky is the limit. But before the ink dries, winds and weather change—rapidly. We endure months of excuses. We keep inquiring as to the reasons for accounts never closing. Chuck doesn't perform but has improbable and eloquent excuses. The people around him dodge and evade. Verdict? Chuck is absent, but not with empty pockets. Over time, a sense of helplessness settles in along with aggressive demands for that damn retainer. A year later, we are $24,000 in the hole and under fifty accounts are closed—all modest, independent, small-performing accounts. Again, a drain of precious operating cash.

3. Ask Potential Brokers to Disclose Their Account Lists

Request that potential brokers disclose their account lists or at least a significant partial listing. Remember, these are supposed to be industry partners, so transparency to some degree can be expected. Make sure you have a clear understanding of any broker's account list. Brokers have connections but not all connections. Be sure they have the connections you need. There's nothing worse than wanting a meeting with Albertsons and your broker doesn't have a connection to get you in. Look over their account lists and see if these accounts make sense to your product's future.

4. Discover How Many Account Executives Are in the Brokerage and What Its Coverage Is

Look at broker staffing levels. If a broker employs ten or fewer people, don't think you will receive nationwide service. I once worked with a broker who claimed their Southern California coverage was stellar. The staffing levels described on their website appeared solid. But what their website didn't reveal was that one of their account executives had quit only weeks before. While we waited for that critical staff member to be replaced, a zero was mounted on our team's virtual scoreboard. This is another form of "broker burn" and is highly manipulative. Be careful of high-turnover broker firms. This is where non-real-time data on broker websites become a problem.

Brokers, like other choice professions, are brilliant at creating strong first impressions. If you have specific retail targets, have your prospective broker call on both the regional buyer and store staff. Broker performance in stores is vital. If your broker indicates they work with Sprouts, visit Sprouts. See firsthand the represented products so you will be clear about the support they provide at a store level and, in turn, whether the store staff will associate your brand with your broker.

5. Ask How Often the Potential Broker Visits Retail Accounts

A focal point of your evaluation should be how often brokers visit accounts. Imagine Raley's has authorized your product to be available in 160+ stores. This can be a worrisome win. You want assurance. This is a moment when a broker should be working overtime. If a broker states they visit accounts every six to eight weeks, that equates to zero feet on the street after such a pivotal success. A brokerage that has lots of staff would be a better choice because employees can visit accounts and buyers with more regularity.

6. Discover How Accessible Buyers Are to You and How Often the Potential Broker Meets with Them

Confirm in advance that a broker can get prior approval for you for meetings. A broker who cannot facilitate meetings? The worst. In this industry, retailer interest dissipates faster than a meteor entering the atmosphere.

Some buyers have no negative feelings about manufacturers attending meetings. Others will deal only with brokers, so you will need to listen carefully to their reports of meetings. If your product is rejected after a presentation, often a broker will dance around the subject to continue billing you while they dodge and evade.

One national firm, Acosta, tends to service more established manufacturers. Acosta has countless connections. They possess a colossal staff of account executives and support staff to sift through new clients. Unlike a smaller firm, they do not court clients. They do not hunt in a traditional sense due to their reputation. When your brand is undeniable, your paths will eventually cross. I warn you that Acosta manages a lot of brands. If you are building your brand you may get lost in the mix and not get the attention you require. However, if you are an established brand Acosta will be an excellent partner and keep business running like clockwork.

Smaller broker firms do have the ability to conquer regions. If you are not yet national, conquer systematically by region. Brokers can give you the specific attention you need to build your brand state by state.

> **M**y rule of thumb is "Pay on performance." Meaning if a broker makes a sale, they get a cut, and if they don't make a sale, they get nothing. This will help weed out your bad brokers fast.

7. Find Out What Other Products the Potential Broker Represents and Whether There Are Any Conflicts

This is a doozy. Michael's Perfect Pickles has five accounts and is considering a new broker company. However, their roster includes several of his direct competitors. This will be a conflict. For example, Hansen's and Zevia share the same broker team. They have always been in competition. They have always fought for the same shelf space. Yet they share the same broker. Go figure.

If you are willing to share space with another successful enterprise, then by all means do so. Some companies have no problem sharing retail space with a competitor. But other companies consider their competitors their nemesis. You decide which one you are: a friendly competitor or a nemesis. Based on that determination you can then choose a broker.

8. Determine Whether the Potential Broker Supports Clients at Trade Shows

Here is an opportunity to develop your relationship with your broker and account executives. At trade shows, your contracted broker should be constantly delivering retail accounts to you to close. They should be literally walking people over to your booth and making introductions. If they aren't, then you are simply enjoying a very expensive, very pointless show.

9. Find Out if the Potential Broker Charges a Percentage or a Retainer

Brokers generally work on a commission of 5 to 8 percent. This would be off the total invoice amount on each order they receive and ship during a calendar month. For example, if your sales are around $5,000 per month, then 8 percent would be $400, which is a lot of money if sales are sluggish. Brokers without minimum retainers will be picky about clients. If a broker is not picky and wants a monthly retainer, this could be a potential broker-burn situation.

10. Outline the Conditions of the Agreement and Termination

A broker's agreement is drafted by you, the manufacturer. The contract is normally two to three pages. Expectations and requirements can be customized in such an agreement. Establish your desired timeline, and particularly be sure to incorporate a termination clause with a short window, perhaps thirty days, and no cancellation fees. Following is an example of a broker agreement:

MICHAEL'S PERFECT PICKLES
Broker Agreement

When fully executed by authorized representatives of the parties, the terms and conditions set forth below shall constitute the whole of an agreement between *Michael's Perfect Pickles* [address, city, state, zip], and [*Name of the Broker*] (hereinafter called "Broker"), and shall become effective [month/day/year].

1. **Scope of Agreement:**
   Broker will aggressively sell specified products of

Michael's Perfect Pickles in accordance with Michael's Perfect Pickles authorized prices and published policies. All orders shall be subject to confirmation by Michael's Perfect Pickles.

2. Normal Brokerage:

Brokerage rate shall be [industry standard is 4 to 6 percent] on net amount of invoice on line of retail and/or food-service products. There will be adjusted brokerage rates on chain account and proprietary products.

3. Payment of Brokerage:

Payment of brokerage will be computed on transactions in the calendar month and made after the closing thereof. No brokerage will be paid on uncollectable accounts. Brokerage will be deducted against all credits issued to any customer, spoilage excluded.

4. Incentives:

Bonus and incentives may supplement this Agreement for periods, under conditions, and at rates specified by Michael's Perfect Pickles.

5. Stipulations:

No like competitive products will be accepted by Broker for his territory without prior clearance and written approval of Michael's Perfect Pickles. No competitor shall be consulted directly or counseled in any manner.

6. **Split Brokerage:**

In the event there are overlapping territories, the brokerage rate will be one half to the Broker soliciting and submitting the order, and one half to the Broker into whose territory the merchandise is shipped.

7. **Broker Certification:**

By executing this Agreement, Broker agrees that no part of brokerage paid would in any manner whatsoever be passed on or granted directly or indirectly to any customer, buyer, agent, or intermediary acting on behalf or under the control of any customer to whom merchandise was sold.

8. **Broker and Buyer Harmless:**

Michael's Perfect Pickles agrees to hold the Broker and Buyer harmless from and against any claim made upon Seller as a result of, or injury from, the use of any Michael's Perfect Pickles products sold to Buyer pursuant to the terms hereto, provided Michael's Perfect Pickles is promptly notified of such claim or injury and is permitted to deal therewith, at its own discretion.

9. **Insurance:**

Michael's Perfect Pickles' liability insurance coverage covers only employees and product quality. Broker is to adequately insure and cover his interest relating to his own employees.

10. Termination:

Either party with written notice of intent may terminate this Agreement. Termination shall be thirty days from date of such notice. Brokerage shall be earned and paid only on orders shipped and invoiced prior to the effective date of termination.

11. Other:

No other conditions are implied or included that may alter or enlarge this Agreement.

12. Territory Limitations:

Oklahoma and/or other specific geographic locations in which Broker would represent your product line.

_____   _____

Michael's Perfect Pickles   Brokerage Name

_____   _____

Michael Jones, CEO   Name & Title

It's important to understand that brokers may and will take 30 to 120 days to complete presentations to all the buyers in the market. And these hurdles must be overcome before your orders are placed for shipment; therefore, *no commissions are due initially until orders are shipped and received.* If you are not an established brand, some brokers demand monthly minimum retainers. This would be in effect until their minimum is met. However, I strongly advise you to stay clear of brokers who require retainers.

7

TRADE SHOWS & TABLE TOPS

A food industry trade show is a critical component for a brand's launch and sustained success. In just three years, 2011–14, U.S. natural and organic food sales grew from $28.1 billion to $42 billion, according to www.statista.com. As a result, conglomerates and retailers are attending natural foods trade shows in search of new products such as yours. The Natural Foods Expo West 2012 reported 60,000+ people in attendance and had more than 3,000 exhibitors. Every year the number increases, and this is the biggest show of the year.

Recognize Trade Show Opportunities

To a wandering spectator, food trade shows are a wonderland of delicious smells, free samples, and visual stimulation. Branded bags are everywhere. But for you they are a place to reach your buyers, retailers, individual store staff, distributor reps, brokers, and retail customers. Expos are three days long, and they can be a real learning opportunity. It can be overcrowded during the major hours, so give yourself enough time to explore.

This can be a lucrative and exciting environment in which to launch your brand. For existing brands it's an opportunity to update packaging and/or launch new items, expand territories, and sell case stacks.

Every show booth has an assigned badge scanner to obtain contact information and input orders. Obtaining new contacts is as easy as scanning attendees' badges; most attendees are willing to oblige. Upon the show's conclusion, one can download contact lists and order history to a portable USB drive. Use all the digital tools at these shows to your advantage!

How to Reduce Your Costs of Trade Shows

There are hundreds of trade shows. Costs for a table or booth at major shows such as KeHE's summer and winter selling shows;

UNFI's winter, holiday, spring, and summer Tabletop Shows; Fancy Food Show; Expo East; and Expo West range from $2,000 to $6,000. You can plan months in advance to keep costs low. On the other hand, if you don't watch carefully you may find yourself spending money not in your budget.

Logistical costs are nearly evil. Be cautious. For example, your materials are sent ahead to a particular trade show. You are pleased to see when you arrive at your booth that your boxes are delivered. Your smile quickly fades when you see a bill for $2,500 for that service. Shop around. Get quotes early. Also, keep in mind that logistics don't set up your booth for you. They simply deliver your booth to you at the trade show. Often you need to hire at least one person to help you set up your booth. This helper can be a local demo person (brand ambassador). The costs don't stop there, though. Your hotel, meals, and brand ambassador will cost upward of $3,000. Budgeting $10,000 for a trade show is not outrageous. It's about average.

Immediately take advantage of all distributors' discount programs. KeHE has various discounts such as one for any vendor with fewer than 300 points of distribution (i.e., 300 accounts ordering product) or fewer than six months' time with KeHE. UNFI also gives a discount for new items with fewer than six months in distribution.

Carefully plan how to be seen at a show. When buyers and retailers have eight full halls of manufacturers it becomes easy to miss one. For example, the Natural Foods Expos East and West offer an array of different types of booths, all at various budgets. Established manufacturers often have elaborate displays, many with numerous working parts. Now you could spend up to $20,000 just for your booth, furniture, and location.

For example, it's true that for extra attention and visibility hanging signage is a proven way to attract people from a distance. Using ceiling signage is something for an established brand that "owns" their retail space. You may not be ready for it now but it could be a future goal.

The New Products section is an economical way to stand out early. A location in this section is only a few hundred dollars and is usually front and center. Buyers and retailers always review this section with notepad in hand, jotting down brand names and booth information. UNFI, KeHE, and Natural Foods Expo shows have stellar New Products sections. Make your new product display clean but with just a little pop of brand personality.

Trade show union labor prices are steep. But you can take a cost-cutting route that can save you as much as $2,000. I suggest bringing as much as you can with you to the show setup. For a much smaller fee than a shipping company will charge, add a couple of bags to your flight. Ship remaining equipment and supplies to your hotel along with a dolly. Often hotels will charge a micro fee to hold a package for a guest.

Hotels? Again, shop early. These can run about $150 to $300 per night. Show-discount rooms might be a little cheaper, but make sure you are happy with the room first. Staying at a trade show hotel is highly advisable. After a ten- to twelve-hour day, time is precious.

Typically, all legitimate trade show hotel deals are offered on the trade show site. But be wary. I once worked with a manufacturer who informed me they had a discount show rate for the Hilton they found on another site. When I called the Hilton, no such reservation existed. The manufacturer was too green to realize this alternate site was a scam.

How to Maximize Selling Potential at Trade Shows

You will need effective and engaging sales sheets, and I recommend you prepare a couple of versions. I suggest one generic version for potential new distributors or possible direct sales. The second version is distributor specific with item numbers. Ensure ingredients and certifications are listed on all sales sheets. Include your contact information and websites as well as Facebook, Twitter, and any other social media connections.

Once the show floor gets busy you will want to work your area. If you have a team, one of you can actively work your booth while others work the floor. Your entire team should focus on making as many contacts as possible. Personally walk people over to your booth. You can even hire extra booth labor. Trade shows are chaotic. Buyers and retailers cannot visit every booth. Make it a mission to target specific retailers and buyers and accomplish it.

Four weeks prior to the show, add to your email signature the particular show name and booth information. Every email you write should have something like this: "See you at Natural Foods Expo West Booth #1234, Hall D!" This is a crucial and ambitious step toward getting new contacts.

Contact every potential retailer and buyer as well as existing customers to inform them you are at Expo and they need to see you there. Set up as many meetings as possible at the show. It's a good time to strengthen your relationships with existing accounts and solidify new ones. Trade shows can be a bonding experience with your buyers and retailers.

Whatever fliers or promotion you want to have outside your booth must be cleared with the show first. I worked with a manufacturer who wanted to promote a celebrity autograph signing at their booth. They gave a pile of fliers to a demo girl and sent her into the crowds. An hour later she came back to inform us she had been shut down. Apparently the manufacturer didn't want to pay the associated fees for this kind of promotion and just went ahead without permission. It happens all the time. But you can't get away with it, so don't do it.

The Big Trade Shows

Each year many trade shows, large and small, occur around the country. In the following you will find descriptions of very large ones that draw thousands of people.

Natural Products Expo West
Deal-making atmosphere: high

Expo West is the most anticipated show of the year! Their attendance is over sixty thousand with over three thousand exhibitors. New products and new relationships, along with legacy brands and longtime partnerships, create an energy that resonates through Anaheim Convention Center and drives the industry forward. The show continues to grow in size as well. Natural Products Expo West now encompasses over 1.2 million gross square feet and houses more exhibiting companies as the natural and specialty foods pavilion continues to sell out. The NEXT New Product Pavilion hosts hundreds of first-time exhibitors and trending products. Beyond the exhibit floor, attendees are encouraged to connect and collaborate by taking part in outdoor events, including a farmer's market at the Fresh Ideas Organic Marketplace, community celebrations at the Evenings on the Plaza, and off-site tours. If there is one show to hit every year, this is the one.

WEBSITE: WWW.EXPOWEST.COM

Natural Products Expo East

Natural Products Expo East presents the organic and healthy-lifestyle industry with thousands of products from passionate manufacturers as well as inspiring and practical education and networking events. The Natural Products Expo East is located in Baltimore, Maryland. Expo East boasts one of the highest numbers of show floor orders.

WEBSITE: WWW.EXPOEAST.COM

KeHE Summer Selling Show

KeHE's summer selling show is an extremely well-attended show. However, this show is not attended by the general public. The people you meet there are all potential deal makers. Sure, it's great that some of them may pick up your product at their local stores, but that's not why you are there. You are there to be in front of the big buyers. I have had tremendous success with sales at these KeHE trade shows, mainly because KeHE shows offer scanners that take orders on the floor. This process made it simple to input new orders, new customers, and data mining. I have had sales in excess of $10,000 in a few days.

The KeHE summer selling show is held annually in early February in various cities throughout the country. KeHE has the best parties of any trade show! This translates to socializing with your buyers and retailers, as well as strengthening the industry.

WEBSITE: WWW.KEHE.COM

UNFI Winter, Holiday, and Summer Tabletop Shows

UNFI Tabletop Shows provide UNFI customers direct one-on-one access to suppliers. Customers have an opportunity to see and sample new items, plan promotions, and place orders. Like the KeHE shows, UNFI also provides scanners for order taking. There are also educational sessions where retailers can gather for information on topics such as customer service, trends, non-GMO issues, and much more.

WEBSITE: WWW.UNFI.COM

Fancy Food Show

The Fancy Food Show is one of North America's largest specialty food and beverage marketplaces. This is the show where distributors and retailers look for specialty and natural products that they may not see at a typical trade show. Sure, there are mainstream products at the Fancy Food Show, but there also is a vast selection of gourmet foods that you have never seen before. It's an exciting place to be!

The Fancy Food Show brings in more than 40,000 attendees from more than 80 countries and regions per show to see 260,000 innovative specialty food products.

Only Specialty Food Association members can exhibit at the Fancy Food Shows. You can see retailers, restaurateurs, distributors, and other innovative new food and beverage products. This show is attended by the majority of the major food-buying channels and the influential members of the trade and consumer press and other related businesses.

WEBSITE: WWW.SPECIALTYFOOD.COM

Trade shows can seem like a circus! No doubt one can make you feel like the tightrope-walking bear. However, they also can get all eyes on you and people wanting you to succeed. These shows are absolutely essential to your success, so maximize them to the best of your ability. It's an investment into your product's future.

FREE-FILLS, DEMOS, ADS, & DISCOUNTS

I have previously mentioned free-fills and demonstrations, tools used to promote products. When you try to place your product with a new account, you will be pressured to provide such promotions and ads and discounts, and if the account doesn't like what you have to offer on an ongoing basis, they make take a loss and send your product off to the half-price bins.

What is a free-fill? A free-fill is a free case of your product. Most retailers require at least a free-fill to test your product. If you sell, then they will keep buying. For example, Michael's Perfect Pickles just got accepted into Clark's Nutrition. The buyer says, "We'll take your product but only as a free-fill." There are a couple of ways to handle this. One way is to send it through their distributor, who happens to be Nature's Best. Michael fills out a turnover and gives Clark's 100 percent merchant chargeback, or MCB. Or, Michael says he'll send the product directly and delivers it to each store himself.

New manufacturers will be expected to provide retailers a free-fill to acquire placement(s). Free-fills are a part of a product's life cycle—like it or lump it. Very few manufacturers can get around this practice. Usually, established brands can avoid free-fills because they have paid their dues. I recall a supplement whose price at retail was $24.99–$29.99 with six bottles per case, so that manufacturer's free-fill was worth $150–$180 retail per store. Multiply that by 170 stores for a major chain and it comes to over $25,000–$30,000. Ouch!

Then after the initial free-fills comes more cash for ads, discounts, and demos.

But sometimes you will need to stand your ground and say no. So how do you strike this balance? How do you get away from the black hole of retailer demands?

SHELF CHECK ❖ 18

Avoid the Never-Ending Discount Train

A new retail account typically expects a 10 to 20 percent OI (off invoice) or MCB discount for its first order or for an agreed amount of time. In exchange retailers will be expected to buy a fair amount of product to support the ads, demos, and sales that should announce the arrival of your new product. Retailers should place your new product on a sales display to introduce the brand. Sales displays sell product via discounts that you need to supply. On top of that cost most major retailers charge for displays and end caps. (An end cap is a small display at the end of a grocery aisle.) In other words, retailers have an interest in creating in-store revenue streams.

The following tips on discounts will help you face up to these demands:

* For the first 90 days provide 15 percent OI with distributors.

* Tie in promotions with the new account.

* Secure as many accounts as possible.

* Hire an industry-based sales director.

For best demo results, insist that stores buy a minimum quantity of product for a demo in return. This trade-and-barter system has been working for thousands of years—use it effectively to your advantage. If a manufacturer is investing, so should the retailer.

Know How Many Demos Is Too Many

In a product's first twelve months, you will want to close more than 500 accounts and double that in the next twelve months. The minute a manufacturer closes an account that is a retail chain, the chain will immediately inquire about demos. The usual request is two rounds of demos in a retailer's top-performing locations. As a rule, you should keep your offer of demos at approximately two per retail location. Only break that rule for special events when customers come in droves, such as a customer appreciation day, Earth Day, or store anniversary. Demos will boost sales, but your product shouldn't depend on demos. Demos are best used for brand awareness, and the introduction and launching of new items. From my experience, I have found that one or two nonperforming demos is not good news. If your product cannot sell through two demos, find out why and restrategize fast.

It is imperative to acquire information from your customers. When a product is demonstrated it is essential that your demonstrators (i.e., your brand ambassadors) collect unfiltered feedback. Collect raw data from day one. And, numbers tell a story. Make sure your data are telling a good story for buyers. Create a demo report sheet for brand ambassadors to record traffic flow, product interest, brand recognition, comments, and sales during demos. All of this seemingly unimportant data could greatly benefit your cause in future deals.

> One might think major retailers focus only on customer-based sales. In fact, they rely on the revenue from all aspects of having the products on their shelves. For example, they receive money from their vendors in various forms such as for ads, slotting fees, free-fills, demos, and discounts.

SHELF CHECK ❖ 20

Remember, Not All Ads Are Good Ads

Retail chains can advertise your product in their chain publication and in their in-store promotions. For example, if you are advertising at Sprouts Farmers Market, over 170 locations will advertise your product in their publication and/or promote it in store. The majority of retailers have these publications so that customers can grab them as they shop. Or an in-store ad will provide As Advertised coupons or special instant savings tags for advertised items. Customers often leave with some of the advertised product or instant savings coupons or tags. An instant discount often sways the mind from maybe to yes.

Hundreds of manufacturers place in-store ads and spike their sales. On the other hand, hundreds of manufacturers place ads and get nada. So how do you spike your sales with your ads as opposed to dropping a bomb? The key is good data. You need to analyze what ads in what locations are producing sales—or not.

The cost for small-chain retailer ads or instant savings tags will range from about $100 to $600. Larger retailer ads for 100+ locations will be at least $600. For retailer ads for 1,000+ locations, buckle your seat belt. But committing to one or two ads is expected. Committing to ads every second month could prove too aggressive.

Major magazine ads in such publications as *Glamour, Us, O* Magazine, and *People* may seem like a good idea. I believe mainstream cosmetic and hair products do quite well in these publications. But when a sales rep from a big magazine comes calling, remember that mainstream publication ads are enormously expensive and cost far more than most retailer ads. A major brand can afford to purchase a one-page ad in *Glamour*. These expensive ads are also in the magazine, rather than in the store. In-store ads are a call to action for an immediate purchase. If you have a natural product, a promotion in the "Paid Advertisement Section" of a major magazine could be a waste of resources. A new brand is often best served by a talented publicist obtaining free press coverage.

I worked with a manufacturer who was published on the

"Oprah Hot List," which is Oprah Winfrey's top seasonal picks in *O* Magazine. For example, Zevia Natural Soda was submitted by a publicist as an "undeniable" product and *O* Magazine thought so too. Soon Zevia went from being somewhat obscure to a household name. But I know another company that paid big bucks to be in the "Paid Advertisement Section" in *Glamour* and *Shape* and it did nothing for sales. In fact, that company is going under.

When Do You Move Away from the Black Hole?

A product completely relying on brand ambassadors, ads, and discounts to sell will fail. A good deal kick-starts a product, and a good product stays after the sales of the first year. This is why wide margins are crucial in the beginning. They will lessen the blow from promotions and various discounts.

It's when you are off deal that you see the real demand for your product.

In your second year, you can continue to run promotions, but should you end the discounts? And, will customers keep buying? It's the age-old question.

What determines whether your product is a hero or a zero? The answer is consistent sell-through, that is, consistent actual sales. If retailers don't see the product consistently moving, it's problematic. One must have sell-through along with case stacks to support demos. But consistent sell-through will be your product's ultimate test. There's no magical date, but I'd say if a product is not selling through within four to five months after placement, it's probably a zero. If a product sells through within the first six weeks of placement, it could be a hero.

Build Your Brand Ambassador Team

Employ a team of brand ambassadors who are completely engaged with your product and brand. For customers, there is nothing worse than receiving a sample from someone who is apathetic. A customer's first experience with a brand should be memorable. Consumers will remember a bad experience, like a soda served warm and flat.

I have sampled products at demos all over the country. I found a vegan mayonnaise this way that's now a monthly purchase. The samples had been perfectly prepared, and they were delicious. The brand ambassador knew the product well and engaged customers. This manufacturer clearly knew their potential customer and sold the product hard. I spoke with their brand ambassador for some time and really felt her brand attachment. I bought a jar and received a coupon for my next purchase. Now I always use this mayonnaise when I make mashed potatoes, potato salad, deviled eggs, or egg salad, and we buy it whether or not it's on sale. This is the impression your brand ambassador should create: that your product is undeniable and everyone needs to know it.

Empower your brand ambassadors. One way you can do this is with competitive pay. Implement sales bonuses and incentives to energize them. I suggest an incentive for brand ambassadors to sell case stacks of product demos. Offer $10 or $20 as an incentive, or a spiff, as they are called. Often manufacturers will offer a spiff to brand ambassadors and distributor and broker account executives who hit a specific sales goal. These incremental deals can really amp up a brand and expand awareness. It's also a way to incentivize distributor and broker account executives to give your brand extra attention and care when they have many brands to oversee.

Cash should not be the sole incentive, though. Be creative. A hungry brand ambassador could be your future salesperson, so excitement and enrollment are key. Enrollment is when your brand ambassadors are completely sold on your product. When brand ambassadors are excited about your product, you get customers who are excited, and sales roll in. Educate brand ambassadors with a one- or two-hour training session. Every brand ambassador should know your product inside out, so provide all pertinent product-related information. Make them a part of your company's mission so that they will become your evangelists.

Create demo kits with a branded, uniform look. You want

all demos to be aesthetically consistent. Within your demo kit include demo reports, marketing reports, and sales reports. Your brand ambassadors are your eyes and ears for your in-store demo—take advantage of the data they provide. Good kits can only help you develop your product and team.

Have your brand ambassador call at least four days ahead of your scheduled demo to ensure that product for the demo has arrived or will be arriving prior to the demo. If there isn't any product or very little, cancel the demo.

With your product established in the market, ask yourself if you are content to remain a smallish, local brand, leaving yourself time to garden, read, play golf, . . . whatever. Or are you planning to spend another 20 years becoming a major regional, or even national, brand? Do you want to partner with investors to handle Kroger when they come calling? Or do you want to sell the brand when it gets just big enough to attract a competitor to absorb?

9

THE GAME PLAN

Stay Small, Get Bigger, or Sell?

S tarting or expanding a business requires money, so how do you get your hands on some? And let's say your product is a hit. What do you want to do—keep working or sell?

Experience and Equity First

Family and friends are a typical source of start-up funds, but with the downside of problems with them if your business doesn't do well. So where else might you go? State and federal agencies have been providing lots of advice, and sometimes money, to folks who want to start a small business.

The ABC television show *Shark Tank* constantly has sales numbers in focus: "What are your sales?" Oh, the awkwardness and pangs of answering truthfully! Numerous wannabe entrepreneurs dance around this pivotal question.

Congresswoman Judy Chu is a member of the U.S. House Committee on Small Business. She is one of the leaders in the small-business economic recovery. Chu has a site to provide information for small businesses (www.chu.house.gov). This site includes links to state and federal agencies that assist businesses and entrepreneurs in securing loans, exporting their products, and contracting with the government.

There are grants, funding, and loan initiatives from the government, such as through the U.S. Small Business Administration (SBA), which wants to invest in the future economy. Its site, www.sba.gov, is perfect for new businesses like yours!

Invest some sweat equity in someone else's business. Specifically, go to work in the natural foods industry—particularly on the manufacturing side. Make a place for yourself in a new natural foods company that is going to grow. And the money? Work toward getting some equity in the company. Trade salary and time for a piece of the action. Of course, that is not so easy to do. Perhaps you are married, maybe have children, or are young, unemployed, and living at home. But starting a new business is going to be about making tough choices anyway, so there's no time like the present. However, I do have a warning about working for someone else for a piece of their equity, so let's look at that next.

Get It in Writing

I helped build a brand, nearly from conception. There was a family-like environment in the company, and we seemed to be good friends. Together we were a small but powerful team. We all did our jobs and we did extraordinarily well. Deals were closing all over the country. Our sales numbers were climbing. However, to my knowledge, no one in the company earned a competitive salary. We all sacrificed higher salaries to build something of our own. The owner indicated that when the company sold we were all going to benefit: "Everyone will receive a piece, right down to the receptionist. You can go back to making your films." I was satisfied with his response. For three years, we labored together. Then a venture capital group purchased the company. However, I received no share of the promised proceeds of the sale, which, rumor had it, was over $20 million. For my $1.2 million annual sales as regional Southern California manager, I was rewarded with only half my promised bonus because the original owners were supposed to pay it. The fact that the company sold because of our high sales made it doubly insulting that I did not get even close to what I was entitled to. So learn from me: A promise isn't a commitment until it's in writing!

Your contacts in an industry are gold—take care in sharing them. If your company has assigned someone to shadow you and is requesting that you disclose all your contacts, that's not necessarily a compliment. It may be a sign they are selling or planning to fire or replace you. Don't let CEOs bully or charm you out of your valuable contacts.

Choices: Selling or Expanding

Picture yourself a few years down the road. You have worked hard, put in a lot of long days. Might you decide enough is enough? You don't want to just stay small and keep doing the same thing. You can decide to sell to get your money out. Or you can decide that you want to expand, and need capital to do so.

However, because finding a buyer and finding investors if you want to expand both use the same process and people, let me discuss them in the context of getting investors to invest in your company.

Be Realistic When Presenting
a Valuation

I enjoy *Shark Tank*, or, as it's called in the United Kingdom, *Dragons' Den*. A common theme on this show is participants overvaluing their company. Contributing factors to this delusional state are endless. I see laziness and I see an unwillingness to learn about basic business management. And, when faced with their own dismal sales numbers (which always tell a story), show participants act shocked.

When entrepreneurs enter a meeting with potential investors and present inflated evaluations, they quickly face reality. How can they be so naive? Often the sad explanation is that company owners along with family and friends have all invested copious amounts of money and have become too emotionally vested in their business.

Another reason for overvaluation is ego. I once consulted for a team that was almost exclusively run by high-net-worth individuals. As often happens, their past successes made them overconfident. Natural products were uncharted territories for them. Unfortunately, their resume and prior successes did not transfer into this brutal industry. I arranged a conference call for them with a major industry investor. He was excited to meet the team, and at first the conversation was just dandy, but that was short-lived. My leaders mentioned closing major chains and popular retailers. My investor contact responded, "What are your sales?" Their answer? "We are selling off the charts, roughly $500,000 per year. Our valuation is north of $30 million." At that moment, I sensed a pain deep in my chest. Certainly they meant to say $3 million, right? Or maybe 30 million . . . pesos?

After the call, I had a private chat with my investor contact. He said, "These guys are high. Are you kidding me? North of $30 million? There was nothing proprietary about that product. Don't ever call me about this company again."

This investor is proven and accomplished in the natural foods industry. Although it stung, he was right. If I had known they would use that figure in advance, that call would not have happened. I reported the grim news to my team, omitting the colorful "high" comment. They didn't understand why they were turned down. *This* is a problem.

After this epic failure at raising capital, I "thought" my team would come around with a more reasonable evaluation. So I brought to the table a venture capital group to help raise capital and evaluate the company properly. I set up a phone meeting with this venture capital group, and the conversation, again, went sour. Again a valuation north of $30 million. I could not believe this was happening again. Ignoring the first investor completely, they attempted the same stunt.

I'll never forget the words the venture capital group said to this ego-driven company: "Your company is too small." Do you know what deflating egos sound like? I didn't either until that call.

It's not a failure if your product isn't selling in the big-box retailers, C-stores, or gas stations. Many important and successful products do just fine in the natural and specialty retailers without the need to expand beyond. However, your company will be less attractive to venture capital and competitor buyouts.

What Investors Want to See

Consider looking for a private investor if you want to expand even further. I know that means sharing control of your baby. But if you want to expand, that can be part of the territory into which you are moving. Most investors in this natural industry want to invest in brands that they can build and sell within three to five years. Investors want a good return on investment and will want answers to their questions. When will they get their money back with profit? How will the investor's exit strategy be structured? In other words, you have to look at their investment using their eyes.

David Bonrouhi and Leslie Lum at Calabasas Capital were kind enough to answer some questions so you can understand the investment from the investor's perspective:

Q: Where do you suggest that start-up, prerevenue-generating companies seek initial seed capital—are there companies you work with and can refer them to?

A: Angel groups (Tech Coast Angels, Pasadena Angels, Maverick Angels), friends, and family.

Q: Who would typically be the best sources of information for these early-stage companies that are well suited to advise on business/corporate operational strategy, accounting, management, capital-raising issues, etc.?

A: Angel groups, attorneys, accountants, and business consultants.

Q: Please explain the various types of capital that you raise for companies, when this capital is needed (e.g., typically when companies make $1 million in EBIDTA), and what are the common structure and fees that investment bankers charge for each?

A: Private equity and subordinated mezzanine debt. Success fee: (1) cash (7 percent of first $5 million, plus 5 percent over $5 million); (2) warrants to acquire up to 2 percent of company at offering price; (3) retainer to offset against the success fee: $35,000.

Q: Please describe when it is appropriate for a company to hire an investment banker to raise capital, or buy or sell a company.

A: If the company has at least $10 million in revenues, they should hire an investment banker if they want to either buy or sell a company or if they want to raise either capital or senior or subordinated debt capital other than just traditional bank debt. If they only want or need plain vanilla bank debt, they do not have a need for an investment banker. Ask CPA for referrals.

Q: In the case of an unfunded sponsor wanting to acquire multiple companies, when is it prudent for them to set up a fund (e.g., a search fund, versus raising money with a PPM [parts per million] to start a fund that is set up for acquiring certain industry-focused companies)?

A: After three successful exits.

Q: When are business consultants/coaches best utilized in the growth process of an early-stage firm?

A: Before the company is ready to raise institutional capital.

Q: What are the most attractive types of companies/industries to raise capital for?

A: High growth, high margins, recurring revenues supported by long-term contracts. Already with at least $10 million in revenues and profitable.

Q: What is the current state of the market as it pertains to capital raising and buy-and-sell-side M&A (mergers and acquisitions)? Any noticeable trends in the market (e.g., private equity firms selling their underperforming companies, high valuations, limited capital for certain industries, capital requirements changing)?

A: Overall activity was down in 2013 by about 20 percent versus 2012. M&A activity at the end of 2012 saw a spike because of expiring low tax rates. Valuations are at all-time highs now because supply of good deals is well below the demand. Overall activity is still down, however, because there are not enough strong companies coming to market. It is also a haves and have-nots world. Many mediocre deals cannot get done. Only the highest-quality deals are going through. Valuations are also high because debt is very cheap (low rates) and easy to access.

Q: What characteristics tend to separate successful companies from those that cannot attain success (e.g., inexperienced management, technical/engineer types at the helm of management with no strategic/operational experience, lack of capitalization, high overhead, business model not competitive in the current market, no clear business plan or competitive advantage)?

A: Strong management team.

How Much Is Your Business Worth? Valuation in a Nutshell

Whether you want to sell out or you want to obtain capital for expansion, you will need a clear idea of how valuable your business has become. There are a variety of approaches to valuation. The real truth is that the price of your business is ultimately what someone will pay for it—it is market driven. However, you do need some figure in your head when you begin to negotiate. Getting that figure can be a bit tricky, so my first advice is to get some—advice, that is. Spending some of the offered purchase price to ensure you don't leave money on the table is not a bad idea at all. But for the moment, let's look at a couple of approaches.

Seller's Discretionary Income

In her *New York Times* article, "Determining Your Company's Value: Multiples and Rules of Thumb," Barbara Taylor looks at valuation from the seller's point of view—which would be your point of view. She suggests using some rules of thumb. For example, if you are in manufacturing and have annual sales in the $1 million to $5 million range, then your business is worth three to four times its SDE (seller's discretionary earnings) plus inventory.

Now that requires a bit of explanation. Taylor examines any expense that is considered discretionary (a conference expense, or even owner salary), extraordinary, nonrecurring (repairing damage from a storm), or noncash (depreciation); adds in the current value of inventory; and multiplies the total by a rule of thumb: a small manufacturing SDE should be multiplied by three or four.

Middle-sized businesses and public companies are typically valued as a multiple of EBITDA (earnings before interest, taxes, depreciation, and amortization). Small businesses, on the other hand, are analyzed and valued as a multiple of seller's SDE, which can be defined as EBITDA plus owner's compensation. For general purposes, SDE is the net income (or net loss) on a given company's tax return plus interest expense, depreciation expense, amortization expense, the current owner's salary, and owner perks. This can be viewed as the foundation of small-business valuation.

> "While there are many factors that help determine an appropriate asking price—including competitive advantages, opportunities for growth and historic financial performance—multiples and rules of thumb can be a good place to start. Several resources are available for obtaining data on pricing businesses for sale, including Business Valuation Resources and BizBuySell.com."
>
> ---
>
> —Barbara Taylor, "Determining Your Company's Value: Multiples and Rules of Thumb," *New York Times*, July 15, 2010, www.boss.blogs .nytimes.com/2010/07/15/determining-your-companys-value-multiples-and-rules-of-thumb/?_r=0.</

Present Value of Future Income

Present value of future income, or PVR as it is called for short, looks at valuation from the *buyer's* point of view. To do that you keep in mind the value of money in a buyer's hand. Money in that hand has interest and investment potential. Let's say you have $2,000 and you invest it for 10 percent interest. So now you can earn $200 in one year. Your $2,000 now is worth $2,200 next year. But $2,200 next year is the same as $2,000 now. One can see why that old saying sticks: "Money in hand is better than money down the road."

But money that arrives in the future has less value. So a buyer will give you less for a second year's earnings from your company that the buyer has purchased. And the buyer will give you even less for the third year's stream of income. So how could a potential buyer articulate *their* expectations so as to have a basis for comparing *your* future income to those expectations? This is where net present value comes into play. There is a mathematical formula that you can use to calculate the value of a dollar in the future. Fortunately, for those of us who are challenged by arithmetic, you can go on the Internet and find websites that do the calculation for you. So if you present a forecast to a potential buyer that your net income next year will be $300,000, followed by $400,000 in the following year, the buyer can calculate what that would be worth in current dollars. You will notice that the websites will ask for an interest rate such as 5 percent or 8 percent. That's a measure of risk. If your buyer wants a low-risk investment like a government bond, they would accept a relatively low rate of interest, such as 3 percent. But your buyer probably will look at your company and see that buying it represents a higher risk, so they will want a higher rate of return. Perhaps that might be 12 percent or 18 percent. So their offer might be to buy X years of income with an expectation that they will earn Y%.

You might argue that your company is worth the present value of five years of income. Perhaps a potential buyer may respond with an offer that shows they are only willing to buy the next three years of income. As I've said, your company is worth what a buyer is willing to pay. And again, to emphasize the risk of overstating your case, if you present a $34 million valuation with $5 million in sales, $500,000 in inventory and payroll, and operation expenses of $1 million per year to potential investors, you might get laughed out of the room.

Now perhaps you want to stay on and build your company worth up to $20 million. This will mean you need to take your product to the next level. It's time to hit the summit. Kroger is calling!

THE SUMMIT

Crossing Over
to the
Mainstream Marketplace

Your hard work is paying off and your brand is recognizable, gaining traction to ascend to the next level. At this point, Michael's Perfect Pickles has an impressive sales director, a couple of brand ambassadors, a few merchandisers, and a lead broker. Michael wants to build his $1.5 million in sales to $10 million in the next two years. To accomplish this ambitious growth in sales, Michael must use new capital to make the big jump from natural specialty stores to mainstream stores such as Kroger, Walgreens, and the juggernaut of stop 'n' go commerce: 7-Eleven.

What works in your favor is demand for natural products. In the big-box retailers such as Target, Kroger, and Publix;

C-stores such as 7-Eleven, Shell, and Chevron; and the natural channels such as WFM, Sprouts, and independent natural retailers, these products are booming. All the market data point to this upward trend and it's a massive one. Working against you are major competitors. To take their place, you must *sell*!

Of course, the question is, Sell to whom? Naturally your thoughts turn to contacting the biggies—visiting head and regional offices. But let's start with the obvious. They are not going to have a sustained interest in your product unless people are buying it in their stores. So, first things first: How will you make that happen?

Think Strategically but Act Logically

It's what you do in individual stores that gets customers buying your product. Those local activities will be carried out by your brand ambassadors and merchandisers. They must be engaged in actions that boost your sales in stores. Brand ambassadors and merchandisers are the lifeblood of any brand because they interact with customers *inside* grocery stores and other retail locations. As *your* foot soldiers, they deal with all the activities involved with new store locations: customer interaction, physical labor/setup, demos, and promotions.

All of this work needs to be managed, of course, but by whom? It will not be your brokers. Brokers do manage products, *including* competing products. However, don't expect them to perform this management function.

It will be your regional sales managers (RSMs). Your RSMs train the brand ambassadors and merchandisers and oversee their day-to-day activities, and together they expand the territory. This new growth will come through small chains, restaurants, hotels, casinos, gas stations, vending machines, and anywhere they can sell your product! Your RSMs must seize the moment to gain complete ownership of their territory. They can't let the occasional "no" slow them down! They won't stop until every possible location in their territory is selling your product. That is the mindset of winners. One must look for the opportunity anytime or anyplace. It's there.

I once worked with a company as an RSM, and I wanted to truly show my extra effort and *never-ending* focus on selling. I wanted a major salary increase the minute I started the job. The only way I could show I was the best was to be undeniable. Undeniable requires thinking outside the box.

I attended a big 7-Eleven trade show in Southern California and took orders for thousands of dollars. I admit many salespeople would've been satisfied with those results and called it a day. However, I was still hungry. The trade show was taking place in a huge casino property. This presented a real opportunity for selling my product to the casino itself. So, I proactively sought out the procurement folks from the hotel while I was there. It ended up being a huge single-location account that drove revenue for the company. That year I made a great bonus!

What About Brokers?

Even if you have RSMs, a critical requirement when transitioning from natural specialty stores to mainstream stores such as Kroger, Walgreens, 7-Eleven, and Safeway is to build and maintain relationships with major distributors such as UNFI, Nature's Best, Core-Mark, KeHE, and McLane. Clear and consistent communication with these distributors is key in order to land the major accounts. Distributors must have your allegiance. This *will* require wining, dining, and schmoozing your distributor and clients. It's all part of the game. You need to schmooze your team from time to time too. Incorporate these strategies into managing your team.

Your team must be ready to support your broker, distributors, and retailers. There is no victory in selling 50,000 units of anything if your supply chain can't fill those orders. All three (brokers, distributors, and retailers) want assurances and *confidence* that if they have a problem with an account in Los Angeles someone is close by to take care of it—fast! There is a reason why firefighters arrive within minutes at an emergency—they are in close proximity to the area they protect. This also makes for a solid bullet point in your sales pitch. For example, "We have Abigail Steinberg in Malibu, pending any issues that may come up. She is our RSM." This is concise. This is clear communication to your business partners that support is nearby—a masterful selling point.

Letting Go

As your company grows you will be faced with a significant challenge, one every small-business owner must confront. You will no longer have time to put your hands on everything that goes on in your organization. Your role will be to work out the long-term strategy and ensure that results being produced match that plan. Upper management has specific roles that I'll outline later in the chapter. But the key task you will face is letting go of the day-to-day activities taking place around you.

Organizing for Sales

Now that I have hammered away at the need for effective local activities, let's have a look at the organization chart in Figure 10-1. It contains the strategic focus: getting business from the biggies. Note that the focus is geographic. These sales efforts must be directed at the targets in their geographic locations: their head and regional offices. Note that other parts of your growing company may be organized around functions such as accounting. But your sales efforts *must be geographic*.

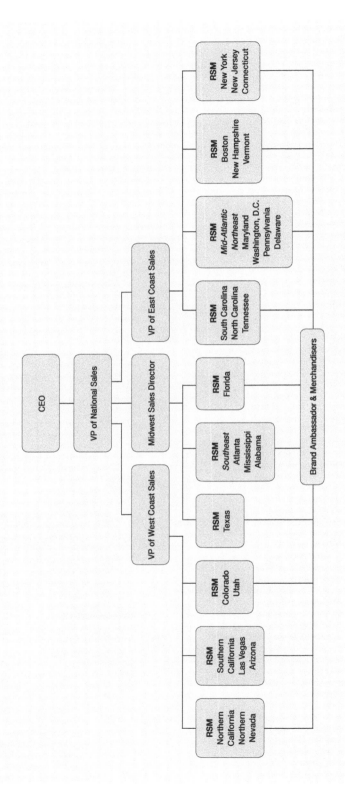

Figure 10-1. Example of a national sales team.

Along with the Advice Comes a Warning

Your sales team needs motivation. People are assets. Develop them to accomplish a *specific* mission. By development I refer to detailed, on-the-job training. You have seen how specific the detail is in this book, such as when describing the demands of a company like Whole Foods. Ambiguity has no place in your operation. And that is particularly true in sales. Asking your sales staff to "sell a lot" is setting an unreachable goal. Selling five case stacks is specific, definitive, and attainable.

The kind of salespeople you're looking for are interesting kinds of people. They have a desire for a piece of the pie for their efforts. So you could offer a bonus program, which is typical in this industry. But be very clear how the bonus structure works. As I said, make the goals obtainable, and establish in advance what the related bonus payoff will be for reaching goals. Rewarding a combination of solid sales performance and new business relationships is important.

On more than one occasion in one company I was congratulated all year round for high sales and new business development. I was the company's champion, and it seemed like every day management would praise my performance. When it was time for the bonus, though, somehow, someway, I just fell short. No bonus. So I encourage you to understand that if all year you promise your sales team a major bonus, you'd better deliver. If you don't, your insulted sales team's enthusiasm will deflate like an old birthday balloon. You don't want your Kobe Bryant of sales to leave your team to sell with your competitor. You want to be tight with costs but you don't want to lose your top salesperson to another team either.

Below I have defined some of the key positions of a national sales team. Please note that all companies are different and responsibilities often overlap. Often these positions are combined due to budgetary reasons.

Senior VP of Sales

The senior VP of sales works in broad strokes. The senior VP lays the foundation of specific strategies. The senior VP also is the one to close national chains, decide on brokers, oversee budgets, forecast sales, create and analyze sales data, and make final decisions about distributors. This *warrior of sales* is the individual who oversees the entire sales team. This individual should inspire everyone in the company.

VP West Coast Sales/VP East Coast Sales

The VP of West Coast Sales oversees the South/West united sales. The VP of East Coast Sales oversees the North/East. These VPs close major regional chains, choose local brokers, report to the Senior VP of Sales and CEO, create regional strategies, analyze and create sales data reports from distributors, and oversee their RSM team. Their job is to educate, motivate, and inspire their RSM team to constantly close sales at chains and service their accounts.

Sales Director

Sales directors are the mentors of the entire sales team. I worked with a sales director who focused on the Midwest and mentored the regional sales managers. Not only did he perform spectacularly in Midwest sales, but he was the glue that kept the entire team together. Sales directors send out sales updates and communicate with operations to ensure stock levels. Sales directors deal with POs to ensure they are filled and sent out in time. They work closely with operations, HR, and the CEO. They are often the voice of the CEO and VP of Sales and in charge of choosing the new hires.

Regional Sales Manager

RSMs are the territory builders in your sales organization. They are your boots on the ground closing the mom-and-pop stores, hospitals, and small chains; manning the trade shows; and training, inspiring, and overseeing their brand ambassadors, merchandisers, brokers, and distributors.

Who Do You Want in Those Boxes?

It's one thing to construct an organizational chart and figure out the duties for each box. It's another thing to get the right people for each box. Building a brand that is a household name requires extraordinary effort by all members of your team. As you look at people to bring on board, focus on their talents in building sales. What can they bring to the table? The masters of sales you want will be persons of established connections *inside* the mainstream market that you are trying to break into. *Who* do your salespeople know? *Who* at _____ do they know? *Who* at _____ have they done business with before? You fill in the blanks.

CONCLUSION

The natural foods industry is important because it can change the way we eat, clean, and consume for the better. This means we need more people like you creating innovative products.

By now I hope you will be able to navigate through the incessantly changing waters of the highly competitive retail world. I do hope that from my hard-won experience you have learned what it takes to avoid common entrepreneur mistakes—and win.

Let me leave you with this: Your journey doesn't end when the product hits the shelf. Instead, it'll always be the beginning because you must continually reinvent your product line, appeal, and approaches in order to become—then remain—undeniable.

I look forward to seeing your product in the store and in my cupboard.

GLOSSARY

Ad Slick

Camera-ready print ads, such as illustrations, company logos, and copy, provided by retailers and manufacturers for newspaper advertisements. Also known as slicks.

Antioxidant

A molecule that inhibits the oxidation of other molecules. The oxidation reactions can produce free radicals. In turn, these radicals can start chain reactions that have toxic effects and cause cell damage. Antioxidants terminate these chain reactions by removing free radical intermediates, and inhibit other oxidation reactions.

As Advertised

A sale price for an item featured in a weekly ad that is lower than the regular price.

Back Order

Out-of-stock items that cannot be shipped with a customer's original order and are sent to the customer as soon as available.

Bar Code

A unique identification code on products, pallets, and coupons. The code is read by an electronic scanner for receiving, ordering, and inventory-control purposes.

Brand

A brand is the symbol that identifies one seller's product as distinct from those of other sellers. The word *brand* refers to the company that is strongly identified with a brand.

Brand Share

A percentage of category sales attributed to a specific product brand.

Broker

An individual or firm that charges a fee or commission for executing buy–and-sell orders for a manufacturer.

Buyer

A person who makes a purchase.

Calendar

A chronological list by month of the major trade shows pertaining to the supermarket industry.

Case Count

A receiving procedure that accepts an invoice's total-order case count instead of verifying the contents of each case.

Category

A division of products or things regarded as having particular shared characteristics.

Category Review

A formal assessment or examination of product with the possibility or intention of including product in schematic.

Chargeback

A manufacturer's bill to a retailer if the retailer fails to meet stated performance requirements.

Direct Sales

A group of salespeople employed by a manufacturing company to work exclusively in promoting and selling its products. Direct sales can also be selling directly via the Internet.

Direct Sales Distributor (DSD)

A full-service distributor who often sells to C-stores and the service industry. However, many DSDs do also service the major big-box retailers and natural foods stores as secondary distributors.

Distributor

An agent who supplies goods to stores and other businesses that sell to consumers.

Entrepreneur

A person who organizes and operates a business or businesses, taking on greater than normal financial risks in order to do so.

Food and Drug Administration (FDA)

The Food and Drug Administration (FDA or USFDA) is an agency of the U.S. Department of Health and Human Services, one of the United States' federal executive departments.

Free-Fill

A free case of product for secure shelf space.

IRMA

WFM database of approved products.

KeHE

International natural product distributor. KeHE is one of the biggest natural product distributors in the world.

Kosher

To be kosher, a product must go through certification and comply with a strict policy of kosher food laws, including cleanliness, purity, and quality.

Merchant Chargeback (MCB)

MCB is a discount percentage that the vendors/manufacturers agree to charge back to themselves through their distributor. In turn, the distributor does not charge the retailer for the agreed-on percentage.

Nature's Best

National natural foods distributor.

Non-GMO Project

A nonprofit organization educating consumers and verifying whether they are consuming genetically modified organisms.

Off Invoice (OI)

A discount is created through the distributor and authorized by the manufacturer. It's often created over a period of time supporting a promotion. Or a continued discount created for a specific buyer or store chain.

Organic
Any food grown or meat raised without chemicals, pesticides, and herbicides.

Promotion
An activity that supports or provides active encouragement for the furtherance of sales for a product.

Purchase Order (PO)
A purchase order is a commercial document and first official offer issued by a buyer to a seller, indicating types, quantities, and agreed-on prices for products or services.

Schematic
A set of approved products in specific space slots.

Sell-Through
Sell-through refers to the *percentage* of units shipped that are actually sold. Sell-through is always expressed as a percentage. *Net sales* essentially refers to the same thing, in absolute numbers. Sell-through refers to sales made directly (direct sales). Sell-in, on the other hand, refers to sales made through a channel.

SPINS

Leading provider of retail and consumer insights, analytics, and reporting for the natural, organic, and specialty industry.

Stock Keeping Unit (SKU)

SKUs are used to manage inventory. A SKU is a distinct item, such as a product or service, offered for sale that embodies all attributes associated with the item and that distinguishes it from all other items. For example, if a brand of pickles has five SKUs, this means it has five different types of pickles.

Super Fruit

A super fruit is considered a new food and beverage product. Super fruits have not been defined by scientific criteria that would allow consumers to objectively assess nutrient value and potential for furnishing health benefits. Consequently, the term *super fruit* is used liberally to include a growing list of fruits having sparse scientific evidence for being "super" other than being relatively unknown to common consumers.

Trade Show

Trade shows are exhibitions for manufacturers in the natural industry to showcase and demonstrate their new products and services. Generally trade shows are not open to the public and can be attended only by company representatives and members of the press.

Turnover (TO)

An order submitted by the buyer, sales rep, or distributor for product sale to a buyer and/or retailer.

United Natural Foods, Inc. (UNFI)

An international natural product distributor. Considered one of the biggest and most successful in the world.

Universal Product Code (UPC)

The UPC, along with the related EAN (International [formerly "European"] Article Number) bar code, is the bar code mainly used for scanning trade items at the point of sale, per GS1 specifications. UPC data structures are a component of GTINs (Global Trade Item Numbers).

Want-a-preneur

Someone who desperately wants to be an entrepreneur but isn't.

Whole Foods Market (WFM)

WFM is an influential national food chain in the natural product industry.

INDEX

ABOUT THE AUTHOR

Abigail Steinberg is both a commercial filmmaker and a successful consultant and senior manager in the natural food industry.

Abigail began her career at Zevia, helping it become the fastest-growing natural product in the country. She has worked as a successful consultant and senior manager in the natural food industry for almost a decade.

Abigail currently resides in Rancho Palos Verdes with her husband, composer/writer Adam Edwards.

Visit her website: www.abigailsteinberg.com